The Internet in Business

Bob Norton and Cathy Smith

TEACH YOURSELF BOOKS

Orders: please contact Bookpoint Ltd, 39 Milton Park, Abingdon, Oxon OX14 4TD. Telephone: (44) 01235 400414, Fax: (44) 01235 400454. Lines are open 9.00 – 6.00, Monday to Saturday, with a 24 hour message answering service. E-mail address: orders@bookpoint.co.uk

British Library Cataloguing in Publication Data
A catalogue record for this title is available from the British Library.

ISBN 0 340 71218 X

First published 1998

Impression number	10 9 8 7 6 5 4 3 2 1
Year	2004 2003 2002 2001 2000 1999 1998

Cover illustration by Neill Menneer

Typeset by MacDesign, Southampton
Printed in Great Britain for Hodder & Stoughton Educational, a division of Hodder Headline Plc, 338 Euston Road, London NW1 3BH by Cox & Wyman, Reading, Berkshire.

CONTENTS

ACKNOWLEDGEMENTS

The author and publishers thank the following for permission to reproduce material in this book:

Admatic; AltaVista; Amazon; American Productivity & Quality Center; Autonomy; Barclays Bank; Bras Direct; Brit Index; Cable & Wireless; CCTA; Davideck; Dejanews; Graphics, Visualization & Usability Center; Hang Seng Bank; InBusiness; InterNic home page reproduction with the permission of Network Solutions, Inc. © Network Solutions, Inc.; Liszt; Nominet; NetPartners; OneLook Dictionaries; Ed Yardeni's Economics Network; Starting Point; Stat-USA; Tesco Stores Ltd; The Business Bureau; The Electric Library; The European Case Clearing House; The Institute of Management; The International Centre for Commercial Law; The Internet Movie Database; The New York Times; The Royal Bank of Scotland; Top Jobs on the Net;Yahoo!

Every effort has been made to contact the holders of copyright material but if any have been inadvertently overlooked, the publisher will be pleased to make the necessary alterations at the first opportunity.

PREFACE

The Internet is making an increasingly significant impact on our lives – at home, at play, at school and at work. It is – in its simplest form – a communications medium which brings together many of the communications tools to which we have become accustomed – telephone, post, TV, fax, video, hifi – all through the PC.

Like all communications tools, however, use of the Internet needs organising, managing and controlling to get the best from it. Nonetheless, like many technologies with huge potential, it is complex in its structure and requires levels of technical expertise in order to exploit it to maximum advantage.

Teach Yourself the Internet in Business is not a technical explanation of how to tackle the equipment, processes and protocols of the Internet. For that reason, it is not necessary to have hands-on experience, nor background knowledge. Nevertheless, if you try out the Internet yourself, or watch others using it, then many aspects will become clearer. You may like to read this book with its companion, *Teach Yourself the Internet*, which describes the technical ins and outs of online working. *Teach Yourself the Internet in Business* is primarily concerned with the management and business issues within an organization. As such, it is written for managers and students who are interested in the effects of the Internet, whether in large, medium or small companies. It does not advocate that all managers jump onto the Internet bandwagon. But it does recommend that all managers should become aware of both the reality and potential of the Internet, because it can change the way we work. Indeed, it can change the work that we do. Some businesses are already deriving benefit from the Internet - success for others to explore, imitate, modify, or reject.

Teach Yourself the Internet in Business introduces the what, how and why of the Internet in non-technical terms, looks at how the Internet grew, explains the kinds of activities that can be performed on the Internet and starts to raise the questions that managers need to consider. It then gets down to the business issues of the Internet and tackles questions of new product development, marketing and selling, security and control, and working out how to fit the Internet to your business.

One caveat: the Internet is moving ahead very rapidly and changing from day to day. As such, a written document describing a dynamic electronic medium is at risk of greater obsolescence than usual. Keeping up-to-date with changes and developments is a must if we are considering the Internet as a business medium. Watch out particularly for new telecommunications developments (Chapter 3) and electronic buying and selling on the World Wide Web (Chapter 9). They are two of the things moving very fast for Internet users.

Bob Norton and Cathy Smith

1 WHY BOTHER WITH THE INTERNET?

1.1 Aims of this chapter

We begin by looking at the significance of the Internet in the current business environment. While there was continuing growth of home use of the Internet in the1990s, business opinion about the value of the new medium was divided. It was a time of popular discovery when not a day would go by without the Press bringing some aspect, benefit or problem of the Internet to our attention. Today, however, there is a general agreement that exploiting the Internet can lead to competitive advantage.

1.2 Business in the 1990s

In 1990, the marketplace and, therefore, business was in a state of discontinuous change and turmoil. Whether the organisation was small, medium or large, the rules of how to do business were changing faster than the ability to cope. This situation was further confused by apparent conflicts between key philosophies. On the one hand total quality management placed a high value on people and on the other, delayering and downsizing viewed them as disposable liabilities. One guiding rule of best practice advised you to 'stick to your knitting' and concentrate on what you do best; another, to re-engineer and diversify in order to penetrate new markets. One set of guidelines advised that market research was still seen as essential for bringing new products successfully to market; another, that speed to market and being first were the only sure-fire way to establish a leading market presence.

The central message was clear however. In order to keep pace with volatility in the marketplace and gain competitive advantage, firms had to exploit new opportunities, acquire new expertise and satisfy customers demanding quality, choice and value for money. In the 1970s and 1980s the underlying business adage had been: 'If it ain't broke, leave it alone'. By the 1990s the maxim had switched to: 'If it ain't broke, break it and start again.' Ways in which organisations began to respond to changes in the marketplace included:

- putting a greater emphasis on innovation and creativity
- building a more flexible workforce
- facilitating greater team-working
- forming alliances with other organisations, even competitors.

1.3 Telecomms and computing

All these approaches were facilitated by the convergence and integration of the formerly separate technologies of computing and telecommunications. This made both internal and external communication easier, cheaper, more flexible and more efficient. This development manifested itself in many forms such as:

- video-conferencing so that people could not only talk to each other at a distance but see each other as well
- computer integrated telephony which links your switchboard to a computer so that, for example, a customer account will appear on the computer screen at the same time as a call from the customer is put through
- call centres which allow companies to operate wherever it is most cost-effective and spare employees the stress of commuting into large cities.

The most well-known and best-used form of converging technologies, however, is the Internet. We shall look at the technological innovations, which have made such developments possible, in Chapter 3.

1.4 The growth of the Internet

By 1990, the Internet had actually been around for 20 years or more, but its use had largely been confined to academic and computer specialist groups in the USA. The next decade saw a huge leap in its popularity and usage to the extent that today it is estimated that home-users and businesses connected to it number tens of millions.

In addition to the capability of formerly separate technologies to talk to each other, this massive growth was down to three main factors:

- the fall in the price, and rise in sales, of personal computers
- the discovery and promotion of the Internet by the media
- the growing user-friendliness of the Internet itself, especially the advent of the World Wide Web in 1993–4.

There were benefits to be had in using the Internet for business – improved and cheaper communications, the opportunity to work more efficiently and effectively from a distance and the chance for companies of all sizes to promote themselves more easily and cheaply to a worldwide market.

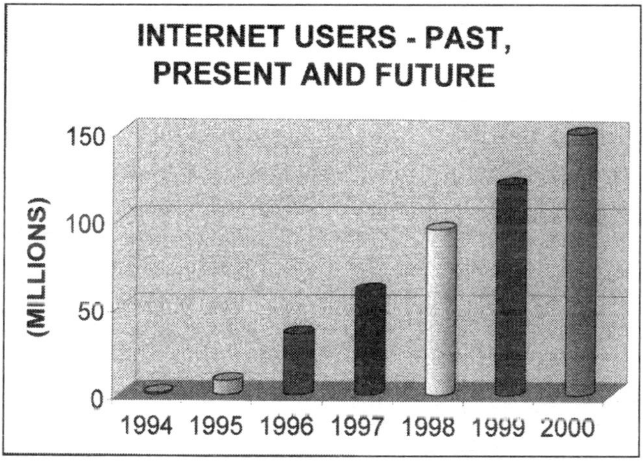

Figure 1.1 Internet users worldwide – a broad indication collated from various sources showing how rapidly Internet usage is growing.

1.5 Attitudes to the Internet

Many businesses, however, fell for inflated promises of an effortless, electronic market where customers would come flooding in. Hype of another kind created unsubstantiated scares that those who were not soon on the Internet would be out of touch and out of business. The result was that, swept along by press articles fuelling hopes and fears, many companies jumped onto the Internet bandwagon, and failed to look at the opportunity as a business project which, like any other, needed thinking about, planning, resourcing, organising and controlling. More seriously, many companies neglected to align and integrate their use of the Internet with their business needs. Consequently many businesses are now asking what they should do next to turn promise into reality, and how much resource they should put into their Internet operation.

1.6 The importance of the Internet

So, after these disappointments, why is the Internet important? Is it just another passing fad, or something worthwhile which can improve the way we work? The answer is resoundingly clear: the Internet is here to stay, it's growing and people's knowledge and use of it are becoming more sophisticated.

The Internet is no longer the preserve of computer nerds. This is partly because the equipment you need – such as PC, modem and appropriate software – is increasingly being packaged as standard so you no longer have to bolt on dozens of different bits and pieces to make it work. It undoubtedly offers an alternative, often a much cheaper alternative, to obtaining, sending, receiving and storing information by traditional methods. We are all in the information business now. Many companies – small and large – are experimenting on the Internet to explore new ways of doing business, including the way they manage their workforce, the way they interact with other organisations, the way they promote their products or services, and the way the buy and sell. Others are using it in a more limited way because they can see no direct return on their investment. The promise of an electronic market, however, is now being reinforced by the investment of major banks and some businesses *are* beginning to derive some bottom-line value. Recent figures suggest that $3 billion worth – and growing – of Internet business transactions are carried out annually in the USA alone.

The Internet impacts on our personal and business lives even if we do not use it. We need to follow debates such as those on:

- the impact of technological progress on business, government and society;
- new forms of marketing and building relationships with customers;

- the social implications of the information 'haves' and 'have-nots' as information becomes a tradeable commodity worldwide and knowledge becomes the key to competitive advantage;
- the legal ramifications of the transfer of information across national borders.

The opportunities – and problems – of the Internet are the subject of debate in the US Senate and the European Parliament as governments struggle to get to grips with the challenges that the Internet poses. The Internet is government business now.

But why do you need to take action now? If there is still so much change going on why not leave it a little longer until it all settles down? The answer is that the Internet is evolving very rapidly. It takes time and effort to investigate its promise and it involves new ways of thinking out how best to take advantage of it. There is, at present, actually little substance for saying that those who leave it late will be out of business, but they will have a lot of learning to do and a lot of catching up while others will have stolen a march. The Internet – and Internet-type technology – is foreseen by many to be *the* business medium of the future.

1.7 What business, what benefits?

To gain a further perspective why growing numbers of organisations are experimenting on the Internet, let us look at some of the possibilities that the Internet offers to businesses:

- The *hotel* business – imagine the cancellation of a block booking leaving your rooms vacant, but in minutes being able to inform particular individuals, companies and agents from far and wide of a special discounted offer.
- The *mail order* business – imagine having your entire catalogue in full colour available to a market of millions without having to deliver it to their door. Imagine too the potential of receiving enquiries and orders 24 hours a day, seven days a week, without anyone having to be there permanently to take them.
- The *writing* business – imagine sending documents anywhere in the world for the price of a local call without having to

print them so that the recipient can continue to work on them without any delay.

- The *recruitment* business – imagine an ad for new personnel accessible by millions at merely the cost of its design.
- The *manufacturing* business – imagine your customers being able to specify – even design – their own model, or variation of it, for you to research and develop.
- The *research* business – imagine market research - without paper, to a specified, or unspecified sample, and being able to minimise the hassle of collecting and analysing responses.
- At *home* – imagine ordering shopping, acquiring software, books and videos, planning holidays, checking the weather forecast, finding out what is going on, even paying bills through the Internet.

Of course, nothing is quite as simple and straightforward as it seems. Such scenarios beg many questions although they are now turning into reality as the benefits of the Internet are becoming more widely understood and appreciated.

MarketStrat – an ongoing survey of the UK online business market – claims that 75% of businesses surveyed were using the Internet for one thing or another. Usage was highest in the academic, media/publishing, consulting and communication sectors, but lower in the food/drink/tobacco and hotel/catering industries. The Internet is beginning to be a market force in the 'information-rich' sectors. But many other surveys project that other sectors are rapidly catching up.

1.8 Summary

The Internet is rapidly developing into a medium which can be used to advantage by business and in the home. Many companies, disappointed with their early experience of the Internet, are now more aware of its potential and are beginning to align it with their corporate strategy.

Using new technology – especially new communications technologies – can help to develop new skills and exploit new business potential. There are benefits to be had for all kinds and size of organisation. Businesses must recognise and embrace change in order to survive and succeed in a climate of rapid development and obsolescence.

2 What is the Internet?

2.1 Aims of this chapter

This chapter tackles some of the most frequently asked questions (FAQs) from those new to the Internet.

- What is the Internet?
- How did it start?
- Who uses it? – growth and user profiles
- How do I gain access and what does it cost?
- What can I do and find on the Internet?

2.2 What is the Internet?

The Internet is an open, worldwide network of computer networks that is interconnected through a mix of private and public telephone lines. The individual networks are owned by a variety of organisations, including government agencies, universities, commercial companies and voluntary bodies that have decided to allow others to connect to their computers – often referred to as servers – to share their information. It is up to each of these contributing bodies to decide what information they wish to make available and how. Along with the computers that store information, there are thousands of others known as routers. These are the ones that keep the Internet traffic flowing.

ROUTER

A computer dedicated to receiving information and sending it on along its route across the networks to its destination.

There is no one single owner of the Internet. The nearest thing to a governing body are voluntary organisations such as The Internet Society or The Internet Engineering Taskforce, although neither of these bodies exercises control in a regulatory or legislative sense.

The most widely used Internet function is e-mail – an alternative to post, telephone and fax. Another is the newsgroups and discussion lists which enable people who are physically remote from each other to come together on the Internet to share and debate common interests. We look closer at e-mail and newsgroups in Chapter 5. The function which has captured the imagination is the World Wide Web, a program which links and retrieves data of all kinds – text, graphics, video, sound – from the inter-connected computers. We shall look at the Web from chapter 6 onwards.

2.3 How did it start?

The origins of the Internet are in the Cold War between East and West in the early 1960s when the US government was searching for an effective communications system in the event of a nuclear attack. The theory was that if vital information were all held in one location, and that location were destroyed, the US war effort would be severely damaged.

As a solution, the Rand Corporation proposed that a decentralised network would continue to work even if some of its components were knocked out. Furthermore, information would be routed around the network not as a complete package, but split into discrete packets that would find their own way through the network and re-assemble at the destination address.

The Advanced Research Projects Agency (ARPA) was contracted to put the theory into practice. In 1969 ARPANET was formed. It linked four universities together using high-speed transmission lines and modems, allowing government scientists and university researchers to communicate with each other by e-mail.

The fast, high-volume telecommunications links between the computers of the participating universities proved robust, and other research organisations and companies began to connect themselves up. In 1973 there were some 40 links in an expanding network. In the same year the UK and Norway connected up via an underwater telecommunications cable. Universities in the USA set up BITNET and those in the UK established the Joint Academic Network (JANET). These networks linked up with ARPANET and the collective grouping became known as the Internet.

A number of advantages were quickly recognised. The ability to send large quantities of data electronically increased the efficiency of information flow. Also, development and use of common communications protocols – known as Transmission Control Protocol/Internet Protocol (TCP/IP) – meant that a computer working on one operating system could be accessed by a different make of computer working on another.

In the 1980s, it was largely researchers and scientists who used the Internet, perhaps no more than about 5,000 people in all and mainly in the USA. As universities connected up, students started using it and when they moved on they wanted the same facilities at work as they had had at university. But the Internet was very 'unbusiness-like'; information was considered to be freely available; the Internet community was close-knit and had established its own communications etiquette.

In 1991 the first commercial service was set up in California – CIX, the Commercial Internet Exchange – to offer Internet access to commercial traffic. But, in the early 1990s, for all but technical devotees, the Internet was difficult to use because it lacked a common interface.

In 1992, researchers in Geneva came up with a way of providing a common PC front-end to Internet computers whatever brand or operating system they were using. This approach also enabled users to switch from one computer to another by apparently seamless links – hyperlinks – and they needed no specialist knowledge or training to use it. This was called the World Wide Web. From then on the Internet has captured the imagination of the press and of business. More than anything else, the Web has transformed the Internet from a community of specialists into a medium now useable by every sector in the community, and in every country with the telecommunications links to support it.

HYPERLINK

The function of switching to another part of the same document or to a different document on the same or another computer by means of clicking on a piece of coded text. On the Internet these hyperlinks are usually indicated in blue.

2.4 Who uses it?

Whatever statistics you believe – and there are a lot of contradictory ones floated about the Internet – the growth in the number of users has been phenomenal.

Latest estimates suggest that there are over 50 million subscribers in the USA, and that numbers are still rising rapidly. European usage is currently put at around 2–3% of all house-holds. German usage is estimated to be higher than in the UK (3 million+ users) with Britain being closely followed by France, the Netherlands, Sweden and then Italy and Spain.

In Chapter 1, we saw an illustration of the rapid growth of the Internet. Pollsters claim that the worldwide community will hit 250 million users by the year 2000. Whatever the estimate – and one has suggested that at current growth rates, everyone on the planet will be connected up by the year 2003 – the Internet is roughly doubling in size every 12 to 18 months.

While this bodes well for business constantly searching for new markets, it is also putting an increasing strain on the tele-communications infrastructure which supports it. Switch on in the afternoon in Europe and communication flow will be a lot slower than in the morning. Why? Because the USA has woken up, and is switching on in its millions.

The early profile of the Internet user painted a picture of the ABC1 35 year-old male described as literate, trend-setting and libertarian, who believes in freedom of speech and the right of every group to be heard. By the mid 1990s this had changed to include the company manager, perhaps in his or her 40s, communicating with customers and suppliers in remote locations and using the Internet to search for and send information pertinent to the business.

Male users still outnumber female – although the gap is closing – and the young and middle-aged outnumber the elderly. The Internet is increasingly penetrating all walks of life, and all age groups, however.

Users are becoming more demanding. Attempts to get people to shop online have been thwarted not only by fears of fraud and lack of security but also by dissatisfaction at the speed of transmission and by boring online shopping catalogues. We'll look at these issues in more detail in chapter 9.

THE GVU SURVEY

One of the most comprehensive user surveys of the Internet is carried out annually by the Graphical, Visualization & Usability Centre of the Georgia Institute of Technology in Atlanta. The GVU survey looks at demographics, usage trends and many related issues. Skip to Chapter 7, Section 7.3 if you want to see more details of this now.

2.5 How do I gain access?

You need a computer that can link to a network that is part of the Internet. Your organisation might have invested in forming a permanent link to the Internet in which case you can take advantage of a permanent connection. Most people's means of connection, however, is to subscribe to one of the organisations which have set up services providing access to the Internet as and when you need it. These firms – Internet Access Providers – offer access to the Internet from your PC via a modem and telephone link, usually to a local number.

This is a very cheap means of using the Internet and is one of many major factors responsible for the Internet's enormous growth and popularity. This is particularly true in North America where local calls are free in some areas.

An Internet Access Provider may charge a one-off signing-on fee as well as an annual or monthly subscription charge. In addition, because Internet traffic is carried along normal telephone lines, you will pay telecommunications connection charges but usually at the rate of a local call, whether your connection is to next door, the next town or half way across the world. We shall look closer at the set-up process in Chapter 4.

There is a further cost – that of your time. This is difficult to predict because it will depend on how hooked you become. On the one hand, the Internet can be an enormous gobbler-up of time. On the other hand, you have to invest time in the Internet in order to understand and assimilate its ways and means – there are relatively few shortcuts. Half an hour per day is a relatively conservative estimate and then there is the time spent reading about it, and keeping up to date with new developments and opportunities.

In the past there have been comparatively few places to actually spend money on the Internet, because payment mechanisms have lacked robustness and security, although odd cases of one-off hackers breaking into systems have generated far more adverse publicity than deserved. This is changing rapidly as people begin to gain confidence in systems that are probably more secure than others we use on a daily basis. More of this in Chapters 9 and 10.

THE TRANSMISSION OF INFORMATION

The modem takes the digital information output from the PC and converts it to analogue format for sending to the local exchange. Most local exchanges in the UK are now digital, so the information is converted back into digital format for sending down the main digital networks in the UK. It is split into packets – each with its common address – which may find their own different route to the destination.

When the packets arrive at the local exchange at the penultimate junction in their journey, they are reassembled for their final destination. There, the information is re-converted back to analogue to go the final distance to the home or workplace. The modem on the receiver's end then re-converts the information back to digital so that it can be received, understood and read on the PC.

2.6 What can I do on the Internet?

There are three main functions that the Internet allows you to perform: communication, information sharing and gathering, and marketing. It is how these functions work and how they are rapidly evolving which makes the Internet a key consideration in the strategy of any business.

Communication

The Internet is mostly used for communication in the form of electronic mail, or e-mail, that permits the transmission and receipt of messages. Each of the millions of e-mail accounts on the Internet has a unique address code which ensures that messages are sent to the correct location. Arrival at the location can take place minutes, or hours, after sending depending on their size, complexity and the distance – and therefore the route – they travel. On arrival they are stored in the e-mail account of the recipient until they are accessed, read, saved or disposed of.

As well as sending messages to those whose e-mail address you know, you can also send messages to special interest groups – newsgroups or discussion lists (see chapter 5) – which exist for the exchange of common ideas, and which can be tapped for valuable information from unknown experts.

Information gathering

While newsgroups can be an excellent source of information, so too is the World Wide Web. Information is available on the Web on every imaginable topic: product and market information, company and financial information, government and economic statistics, library holdings, computer software, videos, weather forecasts – the list is endless. But beware, although this one-stop worldwide information source sounds very attractive, there are several pitfalls and it can be a challenge to find the information you want from the millions of items available. We shall return to this in Chapter 6.

There is, however, another side to the Internet. As well as legitimate, everyday items of interest to all sorts of consumers, anyone can also find the darker side of life with pornography and paedophilia, and subversive material such as how to make bombs, or perpetrate fraud.

Control of 'undesirable' material on the Internet is an even more tortuous question than it is in the real world.

Marketing

Just as the Web is a source of information, it is also the arena for individuals and organisations to market their goods and services. Just as every kind of information is available, every kind of product, service or interest is marketed. Flowers, books and computer software are early success stories.

In six years marketing has perpetrated many mistakes and learned many lessons as it continues to reinvent itself on the Web. Some adverts are very professional, others amateurish, but they all continue to be experimental. The trick is to learn how to keep people's interest and get them to return to your Web pages. We shall look closer at marketing strategies and tactics from Chapter 7 onwards.

2.7 Questions for management

The Internet is an information system of staggering proportions; it can be confusing, frustrating, rewarding and obsessive all at the same time. Before getting hooked up and unleashing the Internet on yourself and your organisation, it is appropriate to reflect on the first considerations of strategy, such as:

- What business are we in?
- What are we really trying to achieve?
- Where are we going and what changes are likely to affect us?
- How does the Internet fit our current and future business?

The short answer to the last question is that there could be gains, or it could be a waste of time. Businesses will have been extremely lucky if gains have been quick and easy. Many have dipped their toes, then feet and ankles into the Internet to find it merely lukewarm and mildly disappointing. Setting up to access the Internet means thinking about how best it can be used – it will consume time and effort to get things right. The Internet should be accepted as an investment for the future, a current cost-centre, a potential profit-centre for the future. But let us delve a little further into the more detailed questions we need to address.

- Why use the Internet? To explore its potential? Learn what it can offer? Curiosity? Fear of getting left behind? Stealing a march on the competition?
- What are we trying to do on the Internet? Exploit the marketing potential? Use a new means of communication? Search databases? Contact experts? Look at company and product information? Explore new markets?
- When should we tackle this? Should we leave it another year as it's still changing shape and style all the time? Or will another year see us left a long way behind with a lot of catching up to do?
- Who should be doing the Internet work? Should we bring in a consultant, hire new staff with Internet skills, or develop ourselves or our staff to learn and tackle what the Internet is all about? To whom shall we allow access? Who has the time? How do we make the time?

- How should we set up access? Leased line, ISDN, or straightforward dial-up? How do we choose a service that provides us with the access that we need and the investment we can justify?

2.8 Summary

We have looked at how the Internet started and developed, at how to gain access, and at what you can do and find when you get there.

The key factor to keep in mind is that if you are going to use the Internet for business, then use of the functions of the Internet must be aligned to your business needs and objectives. The Internet is not just one tool, but many tools in one. It is still changing and growing, and, as such, it can be exciting and frustrating, rewarding and confusing.

Next we look at the technologies which continue to shape and re-shape the Internet.

3 THE COMMUNICATIONS REVOLUTION

3.1 Aims of this chapter

For a long time the promise of a bright technological future amounted to little more than hype from technology pundits. New technology meant high cost and a confusion of systems that didn't talk to each other. It invariably meant a level of risk with little guarantee of return on investment. The Internet is just one of several developments which, as a result of the convergence of formerly separate technologies, are making technology more accessible, useful and cost-effective to organisations. Indeed, in some cases, the speed of these developments has outpaced the ability of many businesses to keep up.

The desktop Pentium processor now has more computing power than entire mainframes possessed 5 or 10 years ago, and at a fraction of the cost. The telephone offers users greater mobility than before and digital telecommunications lines are providing the speed and security necessary for information transmission between remote locations. In this chapter we shall look at those innovations in communications technologies which have made developments such as the Internet accessible not only to larger companies but also to smaller ones – even the home – and focus on the advantages to business.

3.2 Technological trends

The dimensions of technological change have now reduced risk to a level where many of the potential advantages are within the reach of many households let alone businesses. Consider the following:

Power

Microchips are doubling in performance every 18 months to add processing and storage capacity to the PC. *Power* increases in tandem with...

Miniaturisation

An ever-increasing amount of information can be processed and stored on one microchip. This, in turn, is accompanied by...

Cost

Computer prices drop by approximately 30% every year.

Downsizing

There is a shift away from mainframe-based systems with central processing towards PC networks that distribute data across and outside the organisation. The PC is growing into an all-powerful machine.

Connectivity

Network links to the outside world are largely enabled by high-speed modems that are increasingly sold as standard, or by ISDN which needs a special adaptor card.

Volume

More than 13 million computers have been sold in the UK since 1990, the significant growth sector of which has been domestic use. There are over 50 million e-mail addresses worldwide. All UK schools will be on the Internet by the year 2000.

Digitalisation

National and international telecommunications networks are switching to digital to improve efficiency, speed, quality and cost of transmission.

We begin this sketch of communications technologies with the humble telephone.

3.3 The telephone

The telephone is, and will probably remain for some time to come, the first communication tool of business.

Some of us can remember not so long ago that half of Europe was waiting for a dialling tone while the other half was waiting for a telephone line to be installed. Today second telephone lines are offered free of installation charges and the waiting time is zero. Why should we need a second telephone line? Because if you are speaking on the phone, you cannot use that line for communicating from your computer.

But the humble telephone is not so humble any more. Microprocessor chips and telephone handsets have combined to convert the phone back into a slave instead of being a slave driver. Let us first look at some of the developments that are becoming increasingly commonplace.

- Memory storage for regularly-used numbers
- Loud speaker capability to project messages beyond the receiver to enable tele-conferencing
- A call-back number to see who called when you were out
- Remote answer-phone services that you dial into, dispensing with a personal machine
- A caller-display which displays the number of the person calling so that you can decide whether or not to take the call, or leave it for your answering-service, or voice mail. This is a feature of Call Line Identification (CLI) which can link your telephone service to your organisation's customer database. When the customer calls, CLI identifies the origin of the call and the customer account pops up on the screen.
- Call waiting, which lets you know if someone else is trying to get through when you are already on the phone
- Three-way calling – to talk to two other numbers either together or one at a time
- Voice-mail which pages you to dial in to see who called you
- Message relays to divert calls to another number
- Mobile phones, with or without voice-mail, which mean that you can be anywhere at any time and still keep in touch
- Telephony via the Internet where the connection takes place via packet-switching instead of a direct line (see page 14, *The transmission of information*)

Computer technology has helped to regain control over a device which has long interrupted any planned course of events. Just as importantly, the integration of computing and telephony enables distance working to be more effective and allows temporary absence to be less of a nuisance.

All these variations on the standard telephone not only increase the potential for flexible working, but also lead to the 'displacement' of time and space.

They allow the service to be 'there', *without you having to be there*. This is an aspect of 'virtual working' – one of the key benefits of the Internet.

The improvement of telecommunications lines is also a key factor in facilitating flexible and virtual working, which we look at in Chapter 13.

3.4 Telecommunications lines

In order to connect one computer to another, you need a *link*. Within the organisation this is usually achieved through special cabling points on a *local area network* (LAN). On such internal networks, the installation of *structured cabling* enables you to move around equipment such as PCs, printers and faxes without the intervention of specialist staff.

Outside the organisation, telephone lines running through the local exchange into the national and international networks usually provide this link. In the past these telephone lines have functioned adequately for transporting voice data, even text, but they have proved inadequate for the delivery of the content-rich capability that the Internet offers with its mix of text, graphics and video as well as sound. This is because the traditional telephone lines do not have enough *bandwidth*.

BANDWIDTH

Bandwidth is the carriage capacity of the cable. A large water pipe for example can carry far greater quantities of water at far greater speed than a smaller one. In the smaller one any other debris will cause the pipe to become choked up but the larger one will carry it through. With electronic bandwidth a simple colour image may take several minutes to send over the standard telephone lines; a video would probably jam up the lines and never even get there!

You need higher bandwidth to transmit content-rich information effectively.

In the past, if you needed a communications link to carry content-rich information, you could install a leased line. This is a fixed, dedicated external cable that will carry information from one fixed point to another. This can be from one part of the organisation to another, or from the organisation to the local exchange, or to an Internet Service Provider. A leased line will provide much greater bandwidth than the traditional lines but, depending on the capacity of the line, it can be an expensive option to rent.

Now, however, two communications technologies have developed the capability of greater quality and speed of delivery for wider bandwidth requirements, at lower costs than the above options: fibre optics and ISDN.

3.5 Fibre optics

Optical fibre cables are tiny strands of pure glass that carry messages as pulses of light. The copper wires of the older networks are adequate for voice signals but, as well as lacking the bandwidth for image, graphics and video, they are also subject to interference and data corruption. Optical fibres, on the other hand, have almost unlimited bandwidth and are practically immune to interference. They are now installed at major telecommunication junction points and exchanges in the USA, Europe, South Africa and Australia to name just a few of the growing number of countries. It is estimated that, in the UK these optical fibres now carry more than 90% of domestic traffic and 65% of international connections.

Unfortunately, in many cases, the call or signal will still run into the old copper cables between the exchange and home or work and, there, grind to a halt.

3.6 ISDN

ISDN, Integrated Services Digital Network, can be installed by the major telecommunications companies to furnish the final link from the main network to the home or office. ISDN uses digital as opposed to analogue technology and can offer a cheaper alternative to leased lines.

ISDN provides an 'end-to-end' digital service and it can run on the copper wire phone lines installed in most homes and businesses today. It provides the secure and effective transmission of voice and non-voice data on a single network. Furthermore, it can:

- handle multimedia.
- be up to 50 times faster than the conventional telephone lines for text transfer.

- facilitate a new quality in electronic delivery as digital is less susceptible than analogue to interference
- produce connection times which are almost instantaneous, but it also stops the call charge when the line is not being used and starts again when data transfer is taking place.
- allow dial-up: instead of leasing the line, you only pay when you use it. Calls are at the same rate as the standard network, but consume less time, therefore less money.
- enable flexibility: ISDN allows organisations to build their own private virtual networks because communications between remote locations are powerful as well as secure.

An ISDN line normally provides a minimum of two channels with digital capability. The number of channels needed depends on the type, amount and speed of transmission required. Two will be sufficient for a dedicated live video-link and much more besides. The more applications and the more simultaneous usage you intend and the more varied the data transfer you require, then the more channels you will need. Although you will not need a modem, your PC will need an adaptor, or, if you wish to network access to ISDN from a number of PCs, you will need a router.

3.7 Digital capability and business

Leased lines and ISDN may appear expensive, although costs are continuing to drop. They enable applications such as videoconferencing and groupware, however, so weigh such costs against the benefits, in terms of flexible working, easier teamworking and improved speed of information transfer, as well as against alternative costs, which organisations are already paying in:

- transporting people to and from work or for meetings away from the workplace
- office space and equipment
- opportunities and time lost in sending information by mail or courier.

We are, with digital networks, on a vastly improved platform to carry out business activities at much lower costs than before. We explore these possibilities further in Chapter 13.

GROUPWARE

Groupware is software that allows different individuals of the same organisation to share documents easily, to discuss issues and report information, and communicate and collaborate more efficiently. An organisational Intranet is the most recent successful application of groupware technology. We look at Intranets in Chapter 11.

3.8 Next developments

Newer telecommunications technologies are already emerging to provide further options in reliable, high-speed transmission of information. Two of these include:

- Asynchronous Transfer Mode (ATM): a form of data transmission which upgrades ISDN capability for carrying information-rich content, especially video, at very high speed.
- Asymmetric Digital Subscriber Line (ADSL): another high-speed transmission scheme designed for sending (uploading) and receiving (downloading) information at very high speed, although it will require special modems at both ends.

While the telecomms companies continue to explore schemes for speed, reliability and quality to handle ever greater bandwidth, cable and satellite also have great potential to deliver enormous bandwidth. Such is the pace of technological innovation that these technologies will soon be impacting on the way information is transmitted.

3.9 Summary

In this chapter we have looked at how different technologies are coming together to provide an integrated approach to local and distance working.

Medium and larger businesses, which may be engaged in substantial, permanent levels of electronic traffic, might opt to go for a dedicated leased line. ISDN may well be the best type of connection for a small business to consider.

The home user might dispense with the extra cost of ISDN and just use a modem connected through the ordinary telephone lines. Although this cheaper option will lose out on the advantages of speed and reliability, everything depends on the levels of data transmission required.

In the next chapter we look at the issues involved in gaining access to the Internet.

4 GAINING ACCESS

4.1 Aims of this chapter

In this chapter we look at setting up access to the Internet. There are two main ways to do this: through an organisational network and a leased line (this is known as full access), or via a dial-up connection to an Internet Access Provider (IAP).

In this chapter we aim to:

- Describe a full-access, permanent link to the Internet.
- Describe the requirements for, and the pros and cons of, dial-up access
- Describe different types of Internet Access Providers
- Establish criteria for choosing an Internet Access Provider.

4.2 Full access

Your organisation is only likely to go for fully networked access if it has the computing and communications expertise; a fair amount of technical work is involved in setting up and maintaining a permanent link to the Internet.

There are several resource requirements:

- A server of sufficient power and capacity to handle incoming and outgoing traffic for a number of concurrent users.
- A leased line connecting your organisational network to a network on the Internet.
- A router which routes the data signals from your network to others.
- A firewall. This is a computer which sits between the Internet and your computer network. It serves to screen, filter and

select information allowed through to your network and keeps intruders, hackers and anything else unwelcome at bay.

- Specialist staff with the appropriate skills and knowledge to set up, maintain and develop your link.

A computer network with full access to the Internet can benefit from:

- A much faster capability of sending and receiving information because the connection is open all the time and can exploit the advantages of a leased line. The resulting increased speed and convenience leads to a superior electronic mail capability and more efficient information searching.
- Control and independence because you are not dependent on other agencies to supply an access service.

VIRUSES

The spread of viruses through the Internet is a threat to an organisation's information systems.

A virus is usually a malicious program – perhaps injected surreptitiously into your PC or system by means of an e-mail file attachment – which can infect, corrupt or destroy your data or programs, or both. Usually, a virus needs to be set in motion by opening a file; otherwise, it can lay dormant.

New viruses can appear overnight and e-mail attachments – as carriers – remain the greatest threat (see Section 5.6), although there is good anti-virus software available which can offer high levels of protection.

Anti-virus software should be able to scan your whole system, pick up any viruses, automatically remove infected files or do a check of your files to see what damage has been done. Good software should also be able to detect new viruses not yet covered in its portfolio and deny access to the files containing them, thus preventing their becoming active.

There is an independent Virus test Centre at Hamburg University (**http://agn-www.informatik.uni-hamburg.de/vtc**) which monitors the performance of anti-virus software.

4.3 Dial-up access

Usually only large organisations, with substantial and regular needs for rapid information transmission, have a full link to the Internet. Many businesses and most individuals set up access by means of a dial-up connection from their PC to a commercial Internet Access Provider. This is not a permanent connection, and is only active when you dial-up – as in making a phone call – through the ordinary telephone lines (or ISDN). The IAP then connects you up to the Internet.

Equipment

Dial-up access is much cheaper to set up than a full link and much less expertise is needed. Dial-up access accounts for the vast growth of Internet use and almost all access from the home. For dial-up access you will need:

A computer

Almost any type of computer can be used, but most people use PCs, followed – at a great distance – by Apple machines. It is difficult to recommend a specification in such a fast-changing industry. Today a Pentium is standard. It is advisable to have an expandable memory slot that will increase your capacity – and therefore efficiency – in transferring and down-loading files.

A telephone line

This can be direct or via a switchboard. Do have a dedicated socket – especially when many telecomms companies are offering a second socket free of installation charge – otherwise you will have to constantly change the plug depending on whether you want to use the telephone or the PC and the modem.

A modem

Most new PCs have a modem built in as part of the package; otherwise the cost is minimal for attaching an adequate modem. The speed of data transmission down the telephone lines will be enhanced or degraded by the speed of the modem you use. Modem speeds are increasing all the time. A little while ago 28,800 bits per second (28.8kbps) was standard, increased to 33.6kpbs, with 56kpbs also now available. It is important to check that your modem is suitable for connecting to your chosen IAP. If you are installing ISDN, remember that you won't need a modem but a terminal adaptor.

> **TRANSMISSION SPEED**
>
> Transmission speed is a function of the whole connectivity chain, not just parts of it. Even if you have a high speed modem, it won't help if you are trying to capture videos through the old telephone lines. Modem technology is best suited to standard office data transmissions using e-mail and limited largely to text.

Internet Access software

This is provided by your IAP and has all the functionality you will require for using the Internet, including a program for connection, an e-mail package and a browser so that you can search, scan and retrieve information from the World Wide Web. (See Chapter 6 for browsers.)

An account with an IAP

Companies offering access to the Internet have mushroomed. Increasingly though, the market has become so competitive that the services have been more or less improved to similar standards. Choosing an Internet Access Provider is the focus of the second half of this chapter.

Dial-up access problems

Although dial-up access is quicker, easier and cheaper to set up than full access, it does have its problems. It is important to recognise that things will go wrong from time to time – usually when you have something important looming!

- The connection is not permanent, so e-mail does not come straight to you as it does on full access. Incoming e-mail is stored with the IAP, so you have to go and collect it.
- Access can be slow – especially at certain times of the day – when the networks are subject to greater use.
- The host computer of the IAP may go down for maintenance, or it may crash, thus cutting off – albeit temporarily – your access.

Costs

There are two kinds of charges you pay on a dial-up connection:

1. The cost of the telephone call to the IAP. Most IAPs provide access points (known as 'points of presence', or PoPs) to the Internet within local call distance of the majority of homes and businesses, either nationally or regionally. Wherever you 'go' on the Internet, it is the price of a local call.
2. Internet Access Provider fees. Apart from the set-up fee, most providers just offer a flat-rate for unlimited usage. This is typically about £10 to £15 per month.

The cheap flat-rate is attractive and means affordability for many. It also means that you can stay online for long periods of time without running up huge bills. This does, however, have implications for the telecommunications providers who report increasingly congested lines.

4.4 Internet Access Providers

Most IAPs can be described either as backbone providers – offering multiple access points and leased lines, or Internet resellers – which buy space and capacity from the backbone providers to sell on.

Some IAPs have built up specific strengths such as Cix with discussion platforms and UUNet with different types of connectivity (ISDN, leased lines) for corporate access.

Some have developed a strong national presence by demonstrating a capability to develop fast to meet customers needs at the right time and establishing local rate access (e.g. Demon and Easynet in the UK) before this became standard.

In addition to Internet access, some IAPs provide a wide range of extra subscriber services such as access to information, travel, news and entertainment services – for example CompuServe, now merged with AOL, and Microsoft Network – and are international in scope. These are called ISPs – Internet Service Providers. Other ISPs include LineOne in the UK and Prodigy in North America.

Online directories (see *Search engines,* Section 6.5) list up to 80 countries with hundreds of IAPs, but as we have said, there is intense competition in a growing market. It is likely that there will be takeovers and casualties in the future.

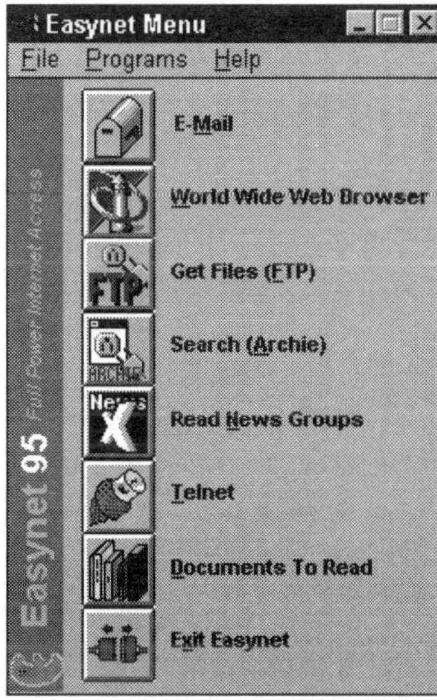

Figure 4.1 Access to the Internet via Easynet: the Options menu.

Figure 4.2 One example of an offer that arrived through the letter-box when drafting this chapter.

4.5 Choosing a Provider

Many people have chosen an IAP through trial and error but save yourself some trouble by listening to the views of friends and colleagues.

1. Find out if the IAP has an established reputation. Ask around or see what the press or Internet magazines have to say.

2. Try out the service at a cybercafe or on a free trial, checking the full fee rates. A fixed price for unlimited access will enable you to budget with more security than an open-ended agreement where you pay by usage. Check that access is available through a local telephone call.

3. Assess the ease of use of the software.
   - How easy is it to install?
   - Can you install it yourself or do you need specialist help?
   - How often is it updated and how are customers informed when it is?

4. Ensure that adequate support is available.
   - How good is the 'helpdesk'?
   - What do other users say?
   - Does the helpline respond in layman's language or do they assume you have an advanced technical ability?
   - What support is offered outside conventional office hours?
   - Is support wholly by e-mail or is there a phone-line as well?

5. Check on shutdown problems.
   - How many maintenance shutdowns take place per month?
   - How many unscheduled shutdowns are there?
   - How long before the system is up and running again?
   - What backup plans are there if the IAP server or leased line goes down?
   - Is any compensation offered for the non-availability of a service?

6. Establish the levels of connectivity the IAP can offer.
   - Can all types of PC platform and all types of modem be supported?

- Does the IAP offer single dial-up access only, or multi-user access?
- Is there a choice of ISDN connectivity? Leased lines? Bandwidth? (see Section 3.4)
- Can the IAP offer upgrading at a later date if improved levels of connectivity are required?

7 Find out if World Wide Web (WWW) space is available if you want to develop your own Web site (see Chapters 6–9).

- Is WWW space included in the annual subscription or is there an extra charge?
- If a small amount of space is free, how much will additional space cost?
- Does the IAP provide training for Web site development? or consultancy?
- What other sites have they set up?
- Can the IAP offer management reports on who is accessing such a Web site?
- Are the reports in standard, readable language or special computer-speak that needs decoding?
- Can the IAP handle sales or forms processing software?

Will the IAP support commercial transactions on the Web?

8 Enquire about your own domain name. The provider will give you an e-mail address, usually in the form:

yourname@providername.organisationtype.countryoforigin

If you are taking out an account for an organisation, ask if you can have an address that reflects your organisation's name. This is referred to as having your own domain name. The provider will charge you an additional fee to register your chosen domain name. We come back to domain names when we look at the World Wide Web.

Internet Access and Service Providers

UK	BT Internet	0800 800 001
	Demon International	0181 371 1234
	Easynet	0171 681 4444
	Uunet (Pipex dial)	0500 474 739
	Virgin Net	0500 558 844
	Cix	01492 641961
	AOL	0800 279 1234
	LineOne	0345 777 464
	Microsoft Network	0345 002 000
Europe	FranceNet (France)	01 40 61 01 76
	Itnet (Italy)	10 6503641
	T Online (Germany)	049 59 990
	GlasNet (Russia)	095 222 0990
	XS4all (Holland)	020 398 7666
	Telepac (Portugal)	1 800 200 079
	Algonet (Sweden)	08 5875 8710
Australia	AusNet	1800 806 755
	Access One	1800 672 395
	Ozemail	1800 805 874
	Microsoft Network	1800 257 253
North America	Prodigy	800 776 3449
	MCI Internet	800 550 0927
	Netcom	800 NETCOM1
	PSINet	800 827 7482
	GTE Internet	800 GTE 1322
	AOL	800 827 6364
	Microsoft Network	800 386 5550
Asia	Pacific Surf (Singapore)	1 800 872 1455
	Pinter (Indonesia)	21 5307830
	VNSL (India)	22 264 1544
	Taiwan	2 344 3143

4.6 Summary

Begin exploring the Internet in a small way, through dial-up access, keeping the larger questions in mind but not applying them too early or too stringently. You need to keep an open mind on those searching business questions of where you want to go and how you want to get there.

It is important to gain a good overview of what the Internet can offer – warts and all – so that instead of the answer 'I don't know', you can offer an informed opinion based on experience. Keep your options open by ensuring that an appropriate and affordable investment is made, which can be upgraded when the need arises.

You can begin your exploration in the next chapter, with electronic mail.

5 ELECTRONIC MAIL

5.1 Aims of this chapter

E-mail is without doubt the main use of the Internet with hundreds of millions of messages sent and received daily. Many users estimate it combines the best features of telephone, fax and traditional mail (called 'snail mail' by e-mail aficionados) all of which, it can, more or less, replace. Its huge appeal is its ease of use, its low cost to remote places (the price of a local call) and the facility to send attachments to text messages by adding graphics, additional documents, even software.

E-mail is offered as a standard feature of an Internet Access package, so you can begin experimenting immediately by sending messages to anyone else on the Internet.

5.2 E-mail and communication

How does e-mail compare to telephone, fax or the post?

- E-mail can be sent at a time convenient to the sender, like a fax, and read at a time convenient to the recipient.
- Unlike a fax, it won't lie around in a post-room or in-tray, it will stay in the recipient's e-mail account (much like an answer-phone service) until they collect it, read it and dispose of it.
- Although it appears an immediate form of communication like the telephone, it does not necessarily exact an immediate reply from the recipient. Some people attribute to it a notion of 'urgency' as they do to fax. On the other hand, it can lie around – in the recipient's e-mail account – for hours, days or weeks.

- Like a telephone call, it is sent along the telephone lines, but is split into packets which may travel by different routes to the same destination. There the packets are reassembled to form the original message that was sent.
- Like a letter (unless a signature is required on delivery) you have no guarantee that e-mail has been delivered, and like letters and faxes, it does occasionally get lost.
- Like a fax, you can send one message to many people with only one copy of the original.
- Unlike a fax, or letter, it is easy to send a reply without re-keying the return address. You have the option of including – or excluding – the original message in your reply.
- Unlike a letter, fax or telephone, you can also send messages to groups of people you don't know. Turn to '*Newsgroups and lists*', later in this chapter (Section 5.7).
- E-mail users do not have to be at home or at work to receive e-mail. They can access their IAP from anywhere to collect their messages.
- An e-mail message is written, like a letter, but tends to be as informal as a telephone call. This can, as we shall see, have bad, as well as good, repercussions.

5.3 How e-mail works

The most economical way of using e-mail for a dial-up user is to access the IAP to collect and send messages, but to work offline (i.e. disconnect from the IAP) to read and write messages.

Each person using e-mail has a unique address, which has several parts to it. For example:

awc@demon.co.uk

is made up as follows:

awc – is the e-mail username, standing, for example, for Arthur William Clark. Mr Clark might equally well have chosen Clarkaw@demon.co.uk

@ 'is found at'

demon – the name of the host computer/IAP on the Internet.

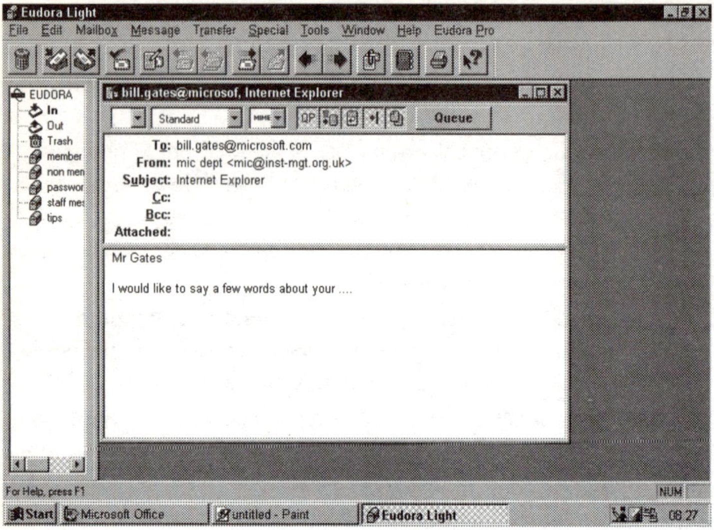

Figure 5.1 Creating a message in Eudora Light mail software: type in the Addressee (in this case Bill Gates...) type your message in the blank space, and click on Queue to send.

co – the type of organisation which owns the host computer. In this case it is *company*, but there are other codes:

- ac – for academic organisations
- org – for non-profit organisations
- gov – for government departments and agencies.

These codes vary from country to country. In the USA ac is replaced by edu.

uk – the country code. All countries have a code, except the USA, because the Internet started there.

Other examples include:

president@whitehouse.gov
santa@north.pole.org
mic@inst-mgt.org.uk

Keep a note of regularly used e-mail addresses. Most e-mail software contains the facility of an electronic address-book, which saves you re-keying addresses and avoids making typos. The wrongly-typed address would result in mail being returned to you.

Netiquette

The Internet has developed an informal communication culture almost eliminating the use of traditional etiquette such as

Dear Mr Smith

Yours truly, sincerely, faithfully.

Many e-mail users take this to extremes, however, making their messages so casual that they are littered with spelling errors and keeping them so brief that they don't make any sense, leaving the recipient to interpret them as best they can!

To overcome misunderstandings that such informality can create, e-mail has developed its own rules and protocols, known as 'netiquette'. One of the main features of netiquette stipulates usage of the lower case. It is considered bad form – SHOUTING – to use UPPER CASE. Other subtleties which the uninformed may easily miss are 'smileys', meant to be looked at 'side-on' and used to give extra meaning to the message, for example:

:-)	the writer is happy
;-)	a wink and a smile
:-D	a big grin
:')	tearful
:-X	I'm keeping quiet about this
:-)8	wearing a bow tie
>:-(	very sad

When there is no face-to-face contact, it can sometimes be easy to cause unintended offence. The smileys help to provide the recipient of the message with the feelings of the writer without use of words. The smileys date from a time when the Internet was a close-knit group of, principally, academics. It is doubtful, however, if the growing business community will bother too much with them, or whether they continue to be in wide usage except amongst those in particular communities. E-mail messages will probably become more formal as business continues to exert its influence.

Other features include abbreviations such as

AISI	As I see it
BTW	By the way
IMHO	In my humble opinion
TIA	Thanks in advance
HTH	Hope this helps
FYI	For your information.

Linking e-mail to old mail

E-mail does not stop there. It is possible to link newer technologies with old. For example, there are services in development which enable you to send a fax via e-mail to those not on e-mail for the same price as e-mail. Such services may also enable you to send a voice message to be delivered as text to the recipient. Others are exploring how the Internet can carry telephone voice messages at much lower prices than the traditional services.

5.4 The advantages of e-mail

- Delivery is faster than traditional mail ('snail mail') and replies can be quicker.
- It is much cheaper than telephone or fax – the cost is not dependent on the distance the message has to travel.
- E-mail overcomes time zone differences and inconvenience, as the recipient does not have to be 'there' to receive it.
- One-to-many messaging is simple and cheap and it enables you to exchange information with people unknown to you.
- With the information in electronic form, the content is easy to re-use.

5.5 The downside

Although there are many advantages to be gained, there are also several dangers to be aware of.

- E-mail is not wholly secure, yet. Anyone can read and intercept your e-mail if they are determined to do so. But it would be unfair to say that this danger is any greater or lesser than with 'snail mail' through letter-boxes. A greater fear is, however, that random surveys show that up to a quarter of the information packets of which e-mail messages are composed can get 'lost' through technical reasons, especially at peak periods when networks are heavily congested.

- Some devotees and advertisers can become a little over-exuberant and bombard you with regular, rambling messages. This can result in masses of junk mail and information overload, which deserves nothing more than liberal use of the Delete key.
- E-mail messages do not arrive on company-headed notepaper bearing carefully constructed logos and a lay-out to catch the eye. Although the sender's e-mail address is included, it is not always easy to identify it.
- There is no guarantee of an immediate response. Some people prefer the telephone if information is needed for a deadline, likening e-mail to sending out a question into a black hole.

  On the other hand, the notion of immediacy might encourage off-the-cuff replies, which might be regretted later. This informality has generated a feeling that e-mail is an unreliable source, lacking permanence, possibly inaccurate, and not worthy of quoting. E-mail is in fact a form of publication, subject to the laws of libel, copyright and the rest. As such, e-mail should be treated in the same way as any other of committing thoughts to print.
- As e-mail becomes more widespread, it becomes susceptible to traditional human foibles and failings. Some managers prefer to hide behind e-mail rather than talk to their staff face-to-face. More alarmingly, some people have been on the receiving end of e-mail bullying, especially by their bosses. Such abuse shows that the cyberworld can carry as many rotten eggs as the real world.
- File attachments to e-mail – software and graphics as well as text – can also contain viruses. The problem is that it is difficult to know whether an attachment is 'infected' or not until it is opened. Given that a virus can wreck the information stored on your computer, some organisations virus-check all attachments before opening them; others ban attachments altogether. (Look back to Section 4.2 for more on viruses.)

- Internet watchers and critics will make much of computer crashes, which put its communications temporarily out of business. Such crashes, when millions of documents fail to reach their destination, occur because some of the major slave computers – check centres, which verify e-mail addresses and route them on – fail. In such cases, the messages are returned to the sender, so they weren't actually lost. They do show, however, that it is unwise to place total faith in e-mail.

S/MIME

One of the latest developments is called S/MIME – an attempt to establish standards for e-mail communication. S/MIME tackles the security problem with two approaches:

You can use a personal digital signature to sign documents. To check signatures you can access an independent certifying authority such as Verisign **(http://digitalid. verisign.com/ query.htm)** or the European Certifying authority: BelSign (**http:/ /www.belsign.be/en/dcc/index.html**)

The second type of security is called encryption – messages are encoded and illegible to anyone who tries to intercept them, (more on encryption in Chapter 9).

At the time of writing, S/MIME is being piloted by several e-mail programs. It represents a key stage in offering business reliability and confidentiality.

5.6 E-mail policy

If you are going to use e-mail in your organisation, you do need to address some policy considerations such as:

1. Reducing the potential for inappropriate use, time-wasting and information overload. Bear in mind that 'inappropriate use' will require definition.
2. Circulation and re-circulation of messages – it is easy to pass on trivia, as well as gold nuggets, at the click of a button. What is acceptable use of e-mail?

3 Reaction – is e-mail to be regarded as more 'urgent' than other forms of communications and if so, how is to be handled?
4 Bullying and defamation – e-mail is a medium for writing and publishing which does not escape establish codes of practice or the law.
5 Responsibility for content – given the power of e-mail to reach so many so quickly and so cheaply.

5.7 Newsgroups and lists

Newsgroups

Newsgroups use e-mail for communication and enable people with common interests to swap views, ask questions and send information and advice. Given that you could come across expertise and opinions which are unknown to you, this can be an ideal place for information gathering and market research.

Newsgroups are grouped under the Internet function of Usenet – a vast collection of some 20,000 groups accessible to everyone who uses the Internet. The uniting feature of each group is a common interest and the means is Usenet's ability to permit an electronic exchange of messages – in 'cyberspace'.

CYBERSPACE

The electronic environment within and across computer and telecommunication systems, and in which information is shared. It is a term coined by the futuristic writer, William Gibson, in his novel, *Neuromancer* (New York, Ace Books, 1984).

This is achieved by sending information to the group's e-mail address; this is then made available to everyone else in the group. You can get everyone else's messages in return. You join up for as long or as short a time as you like as a passive observer or an active participator.

Be aware, however, that some groups receive tens, or hundreds, possibly thousands of messages per day. Depending on the software you use, your Internet Access software will automatically download all the messages for your groups each time you connect to the IAP, or allow you to select only those you wish to read.

Examples of Newsgroups

The following examples give an indication of just some of the thousands of newsgroups available:

alt.education.research
alt.business.seminars
misc.business.consulting
misc.entrepreneurs
rec.music.classical
rec.autos.sport.f1

(*Alt* means alternative, *misc* – miscellaneous and *rec* – recreation)

Here the subject content is more or less apparent from the name of the newsgroup. Others include:

alt.business	schemes for getting rich quick
alt.business.misc	aspects of business and commerce
alt.business.offshore	tax havens
misc.consumers	advice and tips on shopping
misc.invest	managing finance
misc.invest.stocks	tips for the stock market
alt.comp.virus	protection from computer viruses
alt.comp.shareware	software to try before you buy
alt.education. alternative	alternative education schemes
alt.bbs	bulletin boards
misc.legal	various aspects of the law
rec.nusic.info	sources of music on the Internet
alt.energy.renewable	alternative energy
alt.comedy.British	British jokes...

Discussion lists

While newsgroups can come up with some gems, they can also be full of a lot of junk and trivia. Discussion Lists differ from Newsgroups in that they tend to be more specialised and for smaller groups of people. They are often *moderated* which means that the message content is refereed by one or more people who control what goes out to everyone in the group. This is an effective method of screening out undesirable marketing or aggressive opinions, which may not be in the best interests of the group.

Discussion lists provide an opportunity for recognised clubs, groups and committees to keep in touch and exchange their own information.

Examples of Discussion Lists

bpr-l	Business process reengineering
hrnet	Human resources network
learning-org	Learning organisation
leadrshp	Leaders and leadership
management-research	Management research
trdev-l	Training and development

How do you find a newsgroup or discussion list?

One alternative is to use one of the directories or databases, called 'search engines', set up on the World Wide Web. Three in particular are useful for this purpose: DejaNews, Infoseek and AltaVista. More on search engines in the next chapter.

One guide to discussion lists is *The Directory of Scholarly and Professional Electronic Conferences* by Diane Kovacs (http://n2h2.com/KOVACS), available from the United States Assoc-iation of Research Libraries or via the Internet in various forms. A more mundane but perhaps more accurate way is to scan the professional press in your field for listings. Sometimes a commentary on the scope and usefulness of the group is provided.

Internet Relay Chat

With newsgroups and discussion lists, your questions or messages are posted to a common forum or audience and 'sit' there until disposed of, or archived. Newsgroup members can therefore access them at any time.

Internet Relay Chat (IRC) offers 'live' keyboard (and more recently, voice and video) conversations in 'real' time with others on the network. As soon as you enter an IRC discussion, your presence and message are both announced to everyone else currently participating in the group. Those who have free direct connections may often leave their line open all day; this is great for continuous conversation but perhaps wasteful in tying up communications channels.

IRC is available through a number of Internet Access Providers (AOL is particularly strong on this feature) and there are hundreds of open IRC hosts worldwide. Information can be obtained from the **alt.irc** newsgroup, or the Web site

http://www.irchelp.org/irchelp/networks

Although many chat groups may appear breathtakingly trivial, IRC's potential to discuss issues in real time makes it a cheaper alternative to video-conferencing. The implications for staying in touch with colleagues and getting in touch with customers are enormous.

Internet communities

As the Usenet and Chat facilities enable groups of people with common needs to come together in cyberspace, these groupings of people have become known as Internet Communities. Regardless of where they live, the communities share similar interests and – as a group – they can have a growing influence on purchasing power and on the way organisations market their products and services. We shall look at the implications of this in Chapters 8 and 9.

Some of the earlier attempts on the part of commercial organisations to target such communities included deluging specialist newsgroups on the Internet with advertisements by e-mail. This was, and remains, contrary to the informal and anti-commercial nature of such groups and the tactic backfired. The advertisers were swamped (spammed) with so many angry calls and complaints (or 'flames' as they are called by Internet users) that their computers were jammed and they promised not to do it again.

It is perhaps better to use these groups to seek their views on new ideas and to raise their awareness on new developments. When carried out with sensitivity and consideration, newsgroups can be a valuable tool in market research.

5.8 Summary

We have seen how e-mail and newsgroups can impact on the way we work by adding a new dimension to distance communication and opening up new possibilities for current awareness and research. We have also touched on the problems associated with e-mail and suggested ways of mitigating them. Next we look at the World Wide Web.

6 THE WORLD WIDE WEB

6.1 Aims of this chapter

The World Wide Web is a giant electronic information superstore where you can move from department to department easily and quickly and where much of what you find is free of charge. In this chapter we describe this superstore and how to find your way around it.

6.2 What is the World Wide Web?

If information transfer was the fundamental idea behind the beginnings of the Internet, it is the World Wide Web that has done much to reduce the mystery of the Internet and transform it into a useable resource. It is alternatively known as the WWW or the Web, and from humble beginnings it has rapidly grown into a multimedia facility enabling easy, interactive communication, a primary resource for fact-finding, research, marketing, buying and selling. It has captured the imagination as the business medium of the future.

THE WEB

A program which cross references, links and retrieves data from computers around the world using hypertext. This allows you to move within documents, from one document to another or to a document held on another computer without having to turn pages or log out and then log into another computer. These moves are seamless and achieved by using a mouse to click on highlighted words or graphics.

The Web is extraordinarily diverse and you will find information in all forms ranging from gems which would take you ages to find elsewhere, to the banal that you would not want to find anywhere! This is because anyone with a computer, a modem and a little expertise can set up a Web page. With one click of the mouse you can be looking at the thoughts, jokes and holiday snaps of Joe Bloggs, and with a click or two, be sifting through data from the CIA or the UK Treasury.

It is just as easy for small and micro businesses to set up their information as it is for big business – the Web is a great equaliser in allowing large and small to sit side by side. Everyone can be a publisher on the Web and there is no overall censor, editor or quality referee. Wealth, prestige and status are demonstrated by the extensiveness of the site and its quality and sophistication in design.

The Web is a dynamic medium changing all the time; just as owners can update and change the information on their site, they may decide to remove it altogether or replace it with something completely different. Web site contents can and should change very rapidly in order to capture and maintain the interest of visitors. We will look at setting up a Web site in Chapter 8.

6.3 Web basics

Browsers

In order to use the Web you will need a browser. This is a piece of software which sits on your PC and views the contents of Web sites you visit, enabling quick transfer between them through the hyperlinks. It also allows the capture (downloading) of any pages you wish to store on your own PC. The browser is usually supplied by the Internet Access Provider.

There are two browsers that have emerged as market leaders. The first is Netscape, which stole a march on the potential competition, by being free in its early days. The second is Microsoft's Internet Explorer which is supplied as part of the Windows operating system. (At the time of writing, Microsoft is subject to court action in the USA for monopolistic practice in distributing Explorer in this way.) Both are upgraded regularly with new functions and capabilities and both have their devotees and critics.

Does the rivalry between the two major browsers – Netscape and Explorer – matter when a browser is either very low-cost, or included as part of a package deal? The answer lies in the race to become the first common front-end, not just to the Internet, but to all computing activities – on your hard drive, as well as out there in cyberspace.

The illustrations throughout this book show that Netscape (indicated in the top left-hand of the illustration) was used, not in preference to Microsoft Explorer, but because it was convenient.

URLs

All sites found on the Web have an address. You will probably recognise these, as they are now becoming commonplace, signalled regularly in magazines, the press, on radio and TV. Any useful addresses can be stored on your browser; this takes place under Bookmarks in Netscape and Favorites in Explorer.

The Web address is known as a Uniform Resource Locator or URL. This has several parts to it and can be easy to guess or work out. For example, the Supermarket Sainsbury's Web address is

http://www.j-sainsbury.co.uk

This is made up as follows:

http://

Stands for HyperText Transfer Protocol – Web site addresses invariably begin with this identifier although you will not always see this quoted as part of the address as browsers assume its presence.

www.j-sainsbury.co.uk

The name of the server and organisation – and, like e-mail – the organisation type and country code.

The key part of this is the name of the organisation. With millions of people and organisations using the World Wide Web, names can be an important identifier. Some are recognised brand names.

The entrance-hall to the site is usually referred to as the Home Page. The Home Page usually contains the main menu and is thus the key to the site; from there you can readily access other parts of the site using the hyperlinks available. It is possible to by-pass the Home Page, entering straight into the site if you know the exact page address. The screen-shots used in this chapter are principally of Home Pages, but in some examples we explore a site a little deeper as well. To illustrate this we introduce the hierarchical structure of a site, following on from its Home Page.

Some addresses (URLs) may appear long and complicated. They are. Often enough, the information you need may be buried deep in a particular site; the deeper you go into a site, the longer the address.

6.4 A World Wide Web snapshot

These are just a few of the millions of information sites available, although, on the Web, they are not classified into the easy-to-be-found categories that we use here – there is no such order to the Web. Be warned though, that the addresses can change overnight and sites appear and disappear just as quickly. While some sites are completely open access, be prepared for others to require online registration before you enter the site; some are open to subscribers only.

Starting Off

For newcomers to the Internet, there are a number of introductory courses:

TONIC is an interactive online course on all aspects of the Internet offered by the University of Newcastle upon Tyne:

http://www.netskills.ac.uk/TONIC

Introduction to the Internet is also suitable for beginners with links to illustrative Web sites:

http://www.netstrider.com/tutorials/internet

The Start offers a list of links to other sites providing advertising, travel, transport and other goods and services:

http://www.travelbritain.com

The **Confederation of British Industry** has a site, which leads to others of interest to UK and EU business:

http://www.cbi.org.uk

The **British Council** has compiled something similar as a window on British life and culture:

http://www.britcoun.org/direct

The **Institute of Management** is continuously compiling a directory of sites which focus on the skills and practice of management:

http://www.inst-mgt.org.uk

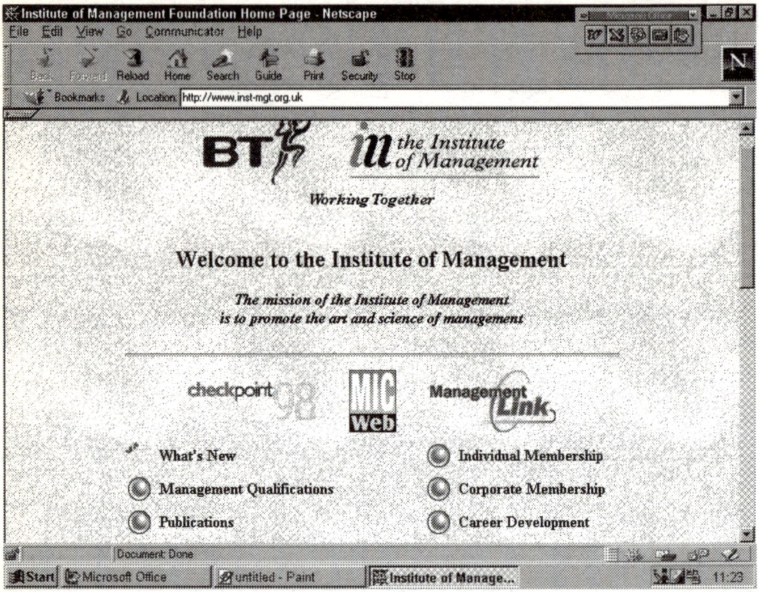

Figure 6.1 The Institute of Management: click on Management Link and skip to Figure 8.5 on page 101.

Reference

Webster's Dictionary with fast if brief definitions:

http://www.m-w.com/dictionary

Eurodicautom translates from one EU language to any other from a database of over 4 million words:

http://www2.echo.lu/edic

A Web-site of on-line dictionaries points to over 300 dictionaries in 100 languages:

http://www.bucknell.edu/~rbeard/diction.html

Onelook enables you to look up a word in over 200 dictionaries at a time:

http://onelook.com

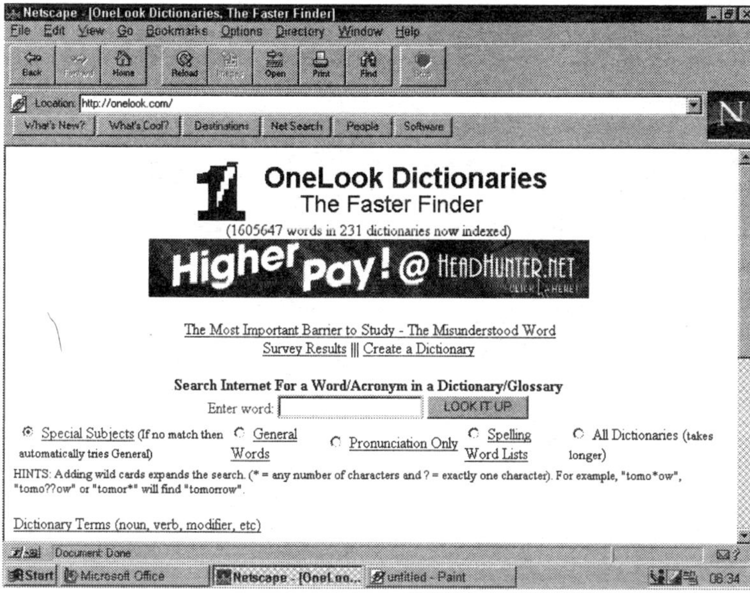

Figure 6.2 Onelook: spellings, definitions and pronunciations from over 200 sources

Findout allows you to submit any question whatsoever on an online form for an expert to answer – at the time of writing, free of charge:

http://www.findout.com

Many other sites are also developing where you can ask questions of a more specific nature such as the **Science Club**:

http://www.halcyon.com/sciclub/kidquest.html

or **Ask Alice** (on health):

http://www.columbia.edu/cu/healthwise/index.html

Selecting books

Online bookshops are among the most successful of early commercial sites. You can often browse/select through thousands of titles and read a review or summary before deciding whether to buy or not.

The American **Amazon** claims to be the biggest online bookshop:

http://www.amazon.com

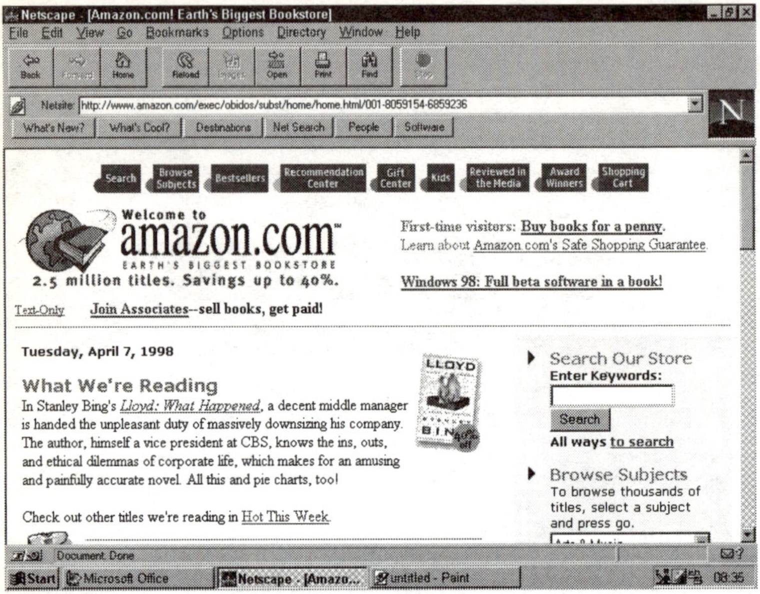

Figure 6.3 Amazon Bookshop: access to over 2.5 million titles for home delivery. For more on this site, see Section 9.5.

In the UK, the Oxford-based **Internet Bookshop** is at

http://www.bookshop.co.uk/hme/hmpge.asp

You can read the reviews from various newspapers, for example, **The Guardian**:

http://www.guardian.co.uk

The **Washington Post** lets you read the first chapter of new books reviewed, free of charge:

http://washingtonpost.com/wp-srv/style/books/front.htm

Business

Dun and Bradstreet offers a database of over 17 million world-wide companies which you can search on their Global Seek site:

http://www.dunandbrad.co.uk/globseek.htm

Thomsons business directories are listed together at

http://www.inbusiness.co.uk

(i)

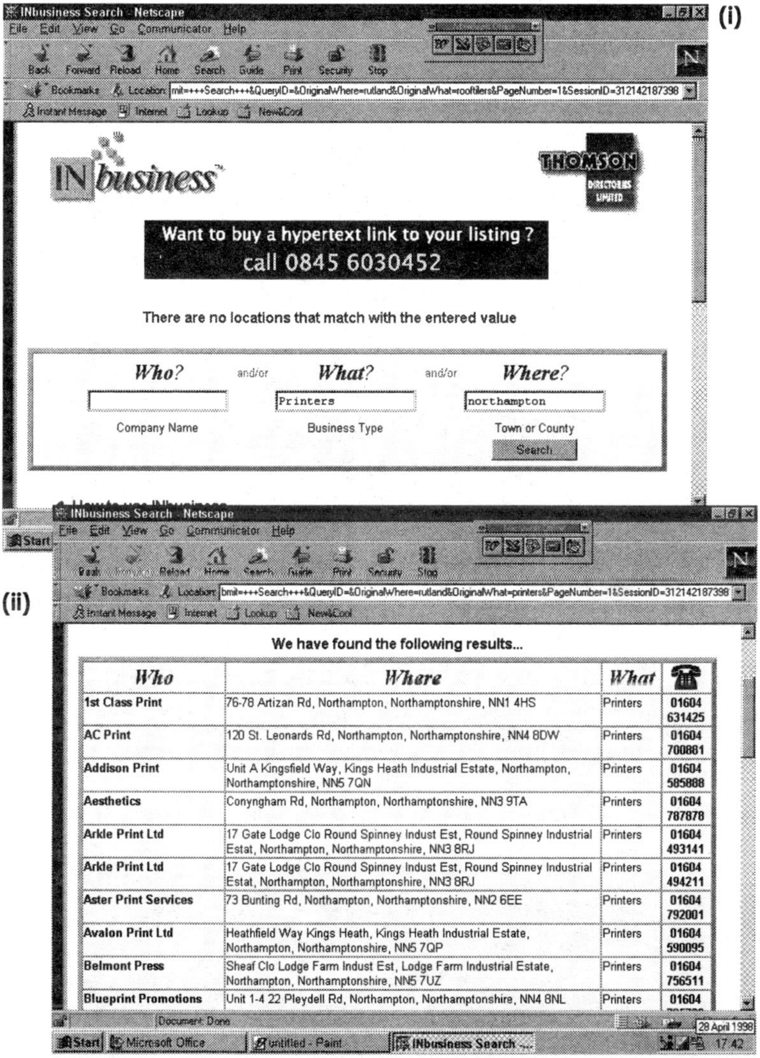

(ii)

Figure 6.4 Thomsons Business Directories: a search for printers in Northampton (i) results in a rapid alphabetical listing (ii).

The **UK Yellow Pages** can be found at

http://www.yell.co.uk

For more on business skip to the next chapter on new product development on the Internet.

Advertising

The Web has a number of sites where you can exchange second-hand goods:

For goods of all varieties, **Free Ads** is arranged into categories which you can break down further to see what is on offer:

http://www.traders.co.uk/ukads

and **Snap** is similar:

http://www.snap.co.uk

Admatic claims to have over 12,000 adverts from all over the world:

http://www.admatic.com

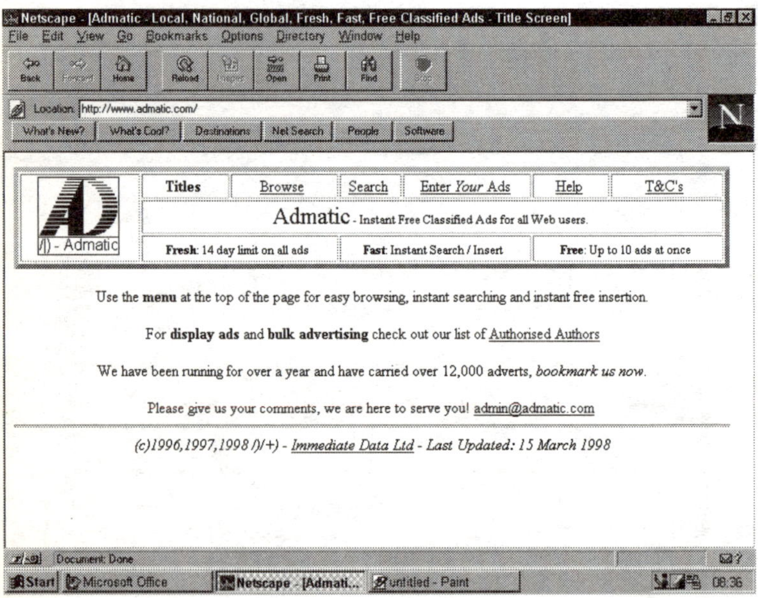

Figure 6.5 Admatic: search for items, or advertise your own, world-wide

For vehicles, there is **AutoHunter**:

http://www.autohunter.co.uk

and **AutoTrader Interactive:**

http://www.autotrader.co.uk

Design

There are sites which enable you to download photographs, drawings and images of all shapes and sizes. They can be identified principally through the search engines (see the following section), particularly Yahoo, AltaVista and HotBot.

Moving Home

Property Sight offer several thousands of houses from many agents throughout the UK:

http://www.property-sight.co.uk

The House Directory offers thousands too and enables you to narrow down your search by region, then area, then district:

http://www.house-directory.co.uk

Jobs

There are a number of sites offering recruitment services and vacancies. Usually, you input your CV, which is either retrieved by or delivered to employers or recruitment agencies:

JobSearch:

http://www.jobsearch.co.uk

JobSite:

http://www.jobsite.co.uk

Monster:

http://www.monster.co.uk

Job Hunter uses regional newspapers as its source:

http://www.jobhunter.co.uk

TopJobs:

http://www.topjobs.net

(i)

(ii)

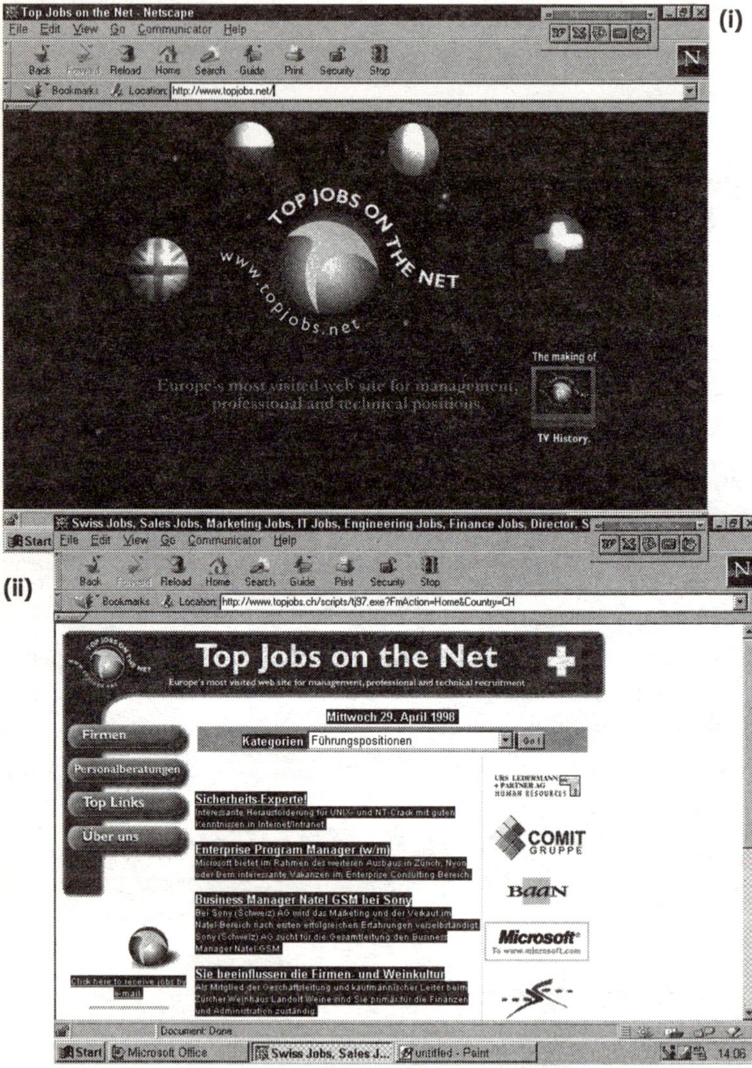

Figure 6.6 TopJobs: a click on the Swiss globe (i) takes you straight into options and appointments in Switzerland (ii).

Government Information

Government departments have become significant promoters of the Internet; many have their own Web sites:

The UK **Department of Trade and Industry**:

http://www.dti.gov.uk

The UK **Treasury**:

http://www.hm-treasury.gov.uk

The UK **Government Information Service**:

http://www.open.gov.uk

The **US Department of Commerce** – an outlet for US business, trade and economic information:

http://www.stat-usa.gov

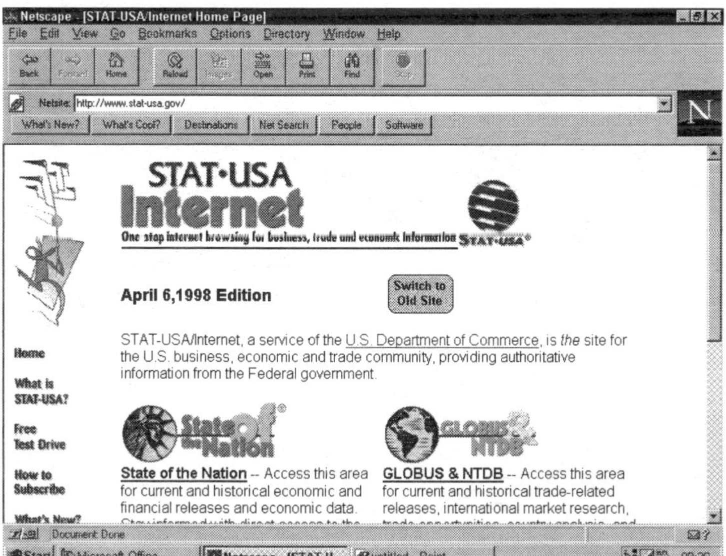

(i)

Figure 6.7 Official US economic and trade statistics from Stat-USA (i). A click on the State of the Nation brings up the Press Releases of the Day (ii).

(ii)

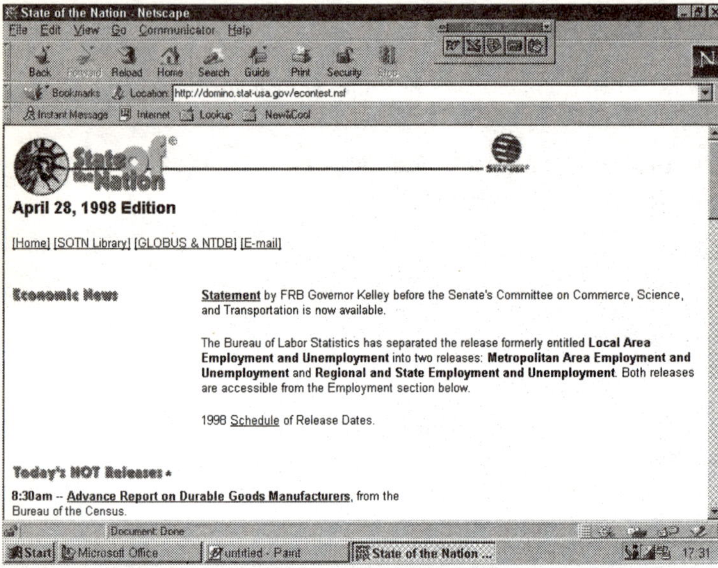

A further click on Durable Goods Manufacturers brings up the text of that Release from the Bureau of the Census (iii).

(iii)

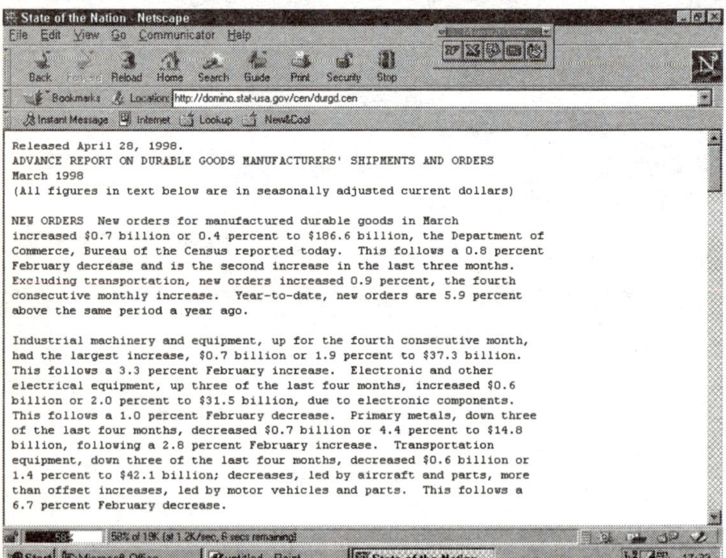

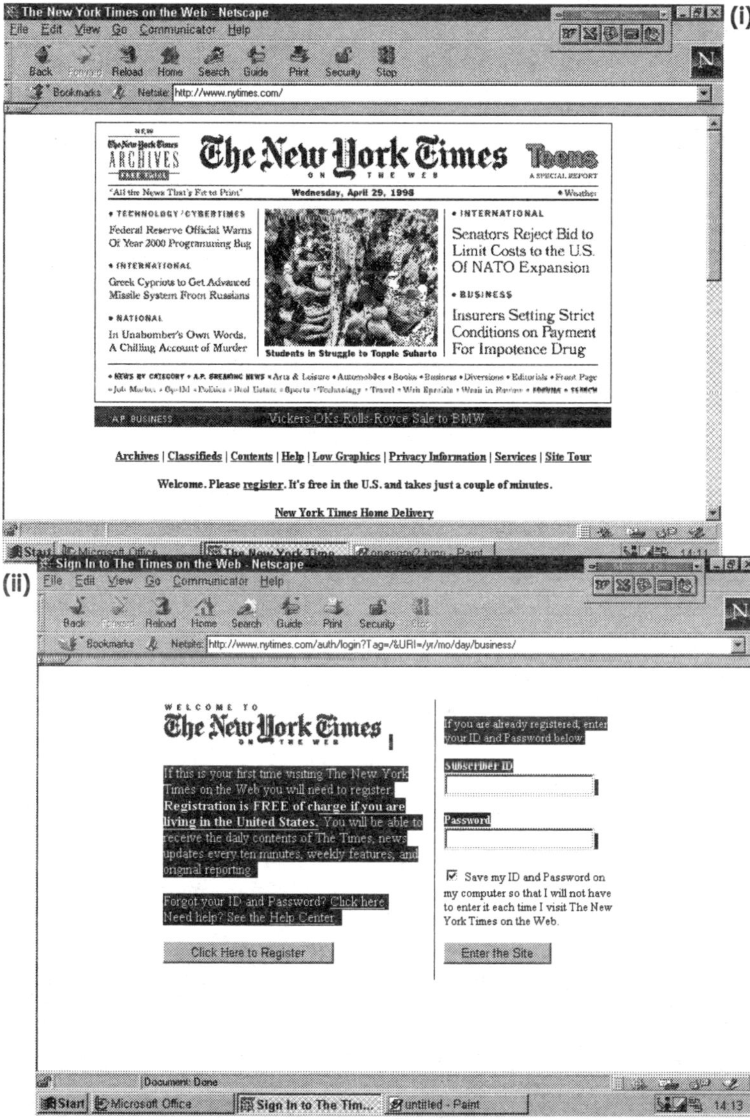

Figure 6.8 As a new visitor to the New York Times site (i), clicking on a news item for further information will bring up a registration screen (ii). This one implies non-USA residents will incur a charge.

Newspapers

Most newspapers now have their pages on the Web. Some let you see just a snippet, some are free, some are not:

The Financial Times:

http://www.ft.com

The Economist:

http://www.economist.com

The Times:

http://www.the-times.co.uk

The Washington Post:

http://www.washingtonpost.com

Le Monde:

http://www.lemonde.fr

The New York Times:

http://www.nytimes.com

Investments

The Web can provides an ideal, real-time source of information on stocks and shares:

EBN, for European stock markets:

http://www.cnbceurope.com

Motley Fool, for checking out the possibilities on Wall Street:

http://www.fool.com

DBC Online, for information on American and some European markets:

http://www.dbc.com

Qualisteam, for an overview of stock market Web sites world-wide:

http://www.qualisteam.com/eng/marche.html

Marketeye, supported by Datastream, allows you to track shares and commodities:

http://www.marketeye.co.uk

Interactive Investor offers a free service to users, setting up details of their investments in unit trusts, life insurance and pension funds. The system can be programmed to send an e-mail message if a given share price index moves up or down by 10%, although it will not allow tracking of individual shares:

http://www.iii.co.uk

All the major stock indexes are available:

Dow Jones Indexes:

http://www.indexes.dowjones.com

Standard and Poor's Index Services:

http://www.stockinfo.standardpoor.com/idxinfo.htm

FTSE indexes:

http://www.ftse.com

Hang Seng:

http://www.hangseng.com/cgi-bin/hsie.cgi

Mathematics & Statistics

The Web is an astonishing source of online calculators, which can help you work out the annual fuel consumption of your car, the interest to be paid back on a loan, a break-even analysis for the accountants, equations and unit conversions. Start off by visiting **The Calculators On Line Center** at

http://www-sci.lib.uci.edu/HSG/RefCalculators.html

which lists, categorises and connects you to hundreds of different types of calculators.

Since the beginning of this book we have talked about Internet usage in the millions and tens of millions. There may be lies, damned lies and statistics, but at least you can check them out yourself on the Web.

Doubleclick collects Web usage data from many Web sites in order to provide commercial marketing information:

http://www.doubleclick.com

Nielsen Media Research is at

http://www.nielsenmedia.com

Leisure and Recreation

London restaurants and pubs:

http://www.uktravel.com/london.html

What's new in **Paris**:

http://www.paris.org

About **New York City**:

http://www.ny.yahoo.com

The **Automobile Association** lists over 8,000 places to stay in the UK and Ireland at

http://www.theaa.co.uk/hotels

CarlingNet – official Web site of the FA Carling premiership:

http://www.fa-premier.com

The **Internet Movie Database** for all you ever want to know about movies:

http://uk.imdb.com

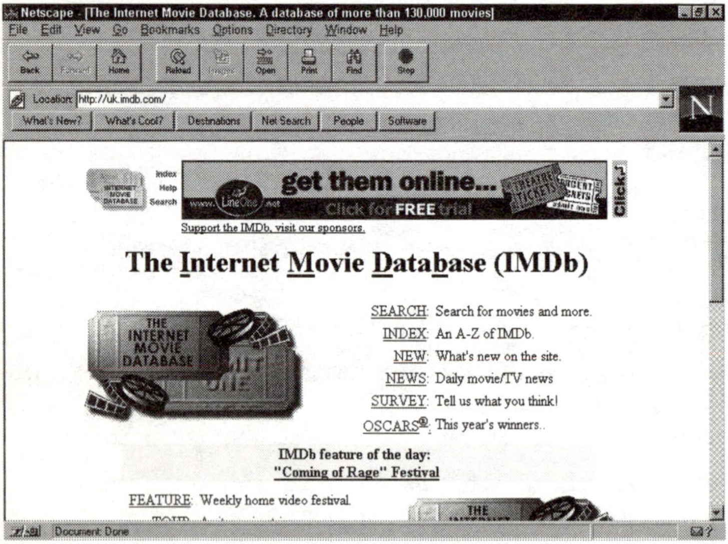

Figure 6.10 The Internet Movie Database for film news and reviews.

The **UK Weather**

http://www.meto.gov.uk

(i)

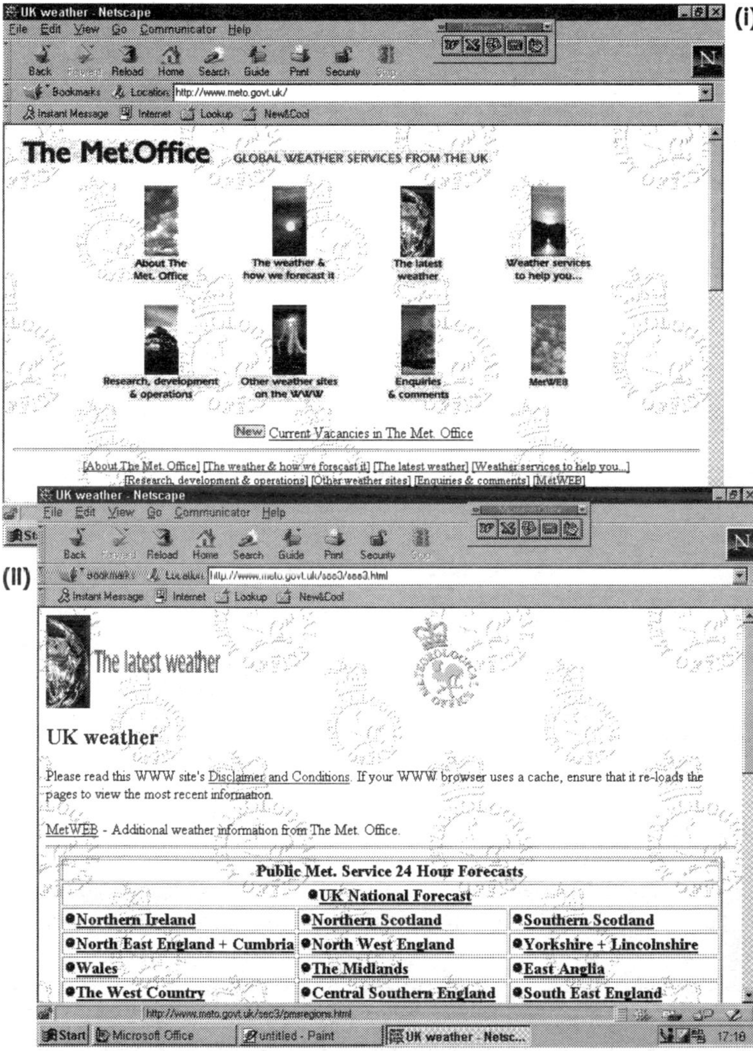

(ii)

Figure 6.11 The Met Office: the latest weather is available on a global scale (i). For the UK, you can select regionally or nationally (ii), although, as we see, it's the usual story (iii).

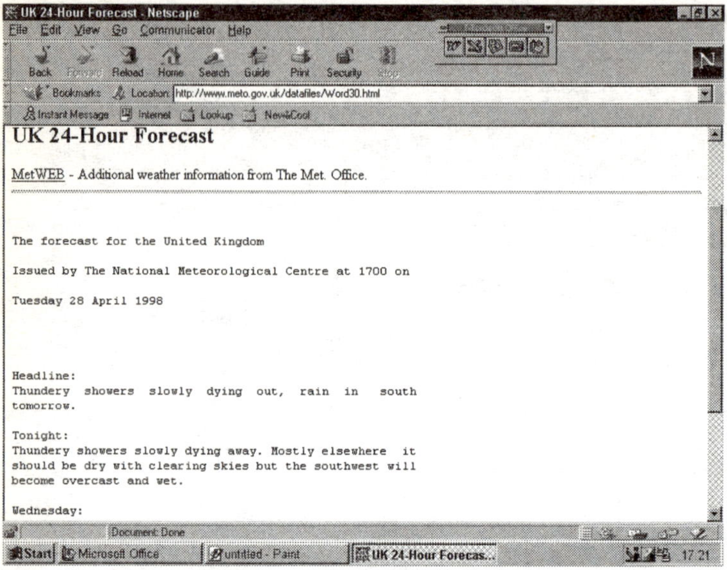

(iii)

6.5 Finding your way around

It is the sheer quantity and varied quality that makes pinpointing specific items difficult. Web addresses can be picked up everywhere – through the media, from friends, colleagues, radio and TV. When you find useful sites, store the addresses on your browser for re-use. It's OK if you know the address, but what do you do if you don't or can't guess it, and you need to search by subject?

One solution is to locate a site that specialises in building subject links to others. Such sites can act as gateways to information of related interest. Organisations adopting this approach include the **University of Nijenrode** in the Netherlands (http://www.library.nijenrode.nl/introduction.html) which is compiling a list of useful business information sources, and the **Institute of Management** (http://www.inst-mgt.org.uk/external/mgt-link.html) which is building links to sites of management interest (see Section 8.3.9, page 100). Usually the links have undergone some kind of evaluation that helps in the search for information of value.

Another answer is to use tools that index all the sites on the Web. These tools include directories and search engines. Directories are compiled by people who index new material on the Web on a continuing basis. Search engines are automated programs that continually trawl the Web for new sites and add the reference to, and location of, their contents to a database. Although directories may be selective, search engines are not and make no distinction between trivia and quality.

The term search engine is the one increasingly adopted for all kinds of search tool on the Web and there are hundreds of them. They vary in speed and efficiency and some have special features to help you pin down the information you are after. While it is advisable to try two or three to gain a good overview of what is available, the more you try, the more information you will have to cope with. A search on a general term like small business will produce thousands of references, or hits. The more precise you can be, the better the chance of striking gold. For more detailed hints on searching techniques, refer to the companion book *Teach Yourself the Internet*. Here are some of the search engines that are frequently used.

Search Engines

Yahoo!

Yahoo! – Yet Another Hierarchical Organized Oracle – is probably the best-known search engine (http://www.yahoo.com). There are various national derivatives from the US original (e.g. http://www.yahoo.fr) and a page that links directly to business sites (http://www.yahoo.com/business).

A special section is devoted to pictures (http://www.yahoo.com/Computers_and_Internet/Multimedia/Pictures).

Excite

This large search engine (http://www.excite.com or http://www.excite.co.uk for the UK) can access over 50 million addresses. It has good UK coverage and allows you to track particular search topics and tailors new information to your specifications.

Infoseek

Infoseek (http://www.infoseek.com) eliminates duplicate hits from more than 100 million pages and has a specific UK directory.

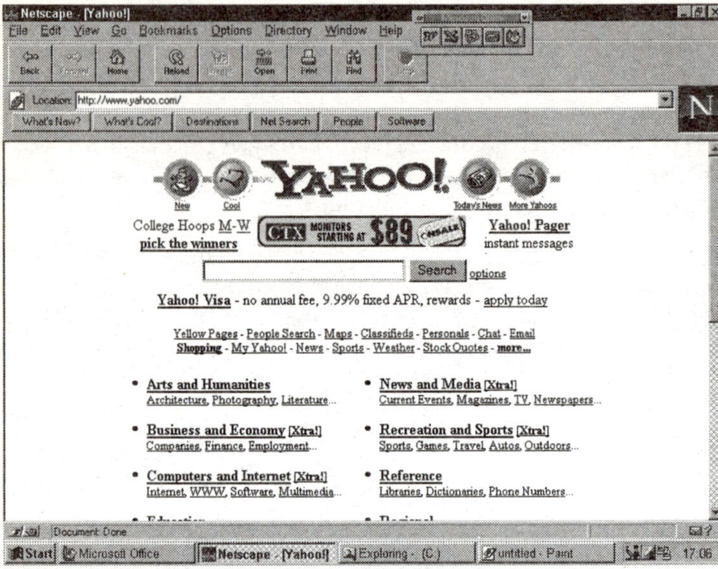

Figure 6.12 Yahoo – a popular starting-point for searches.

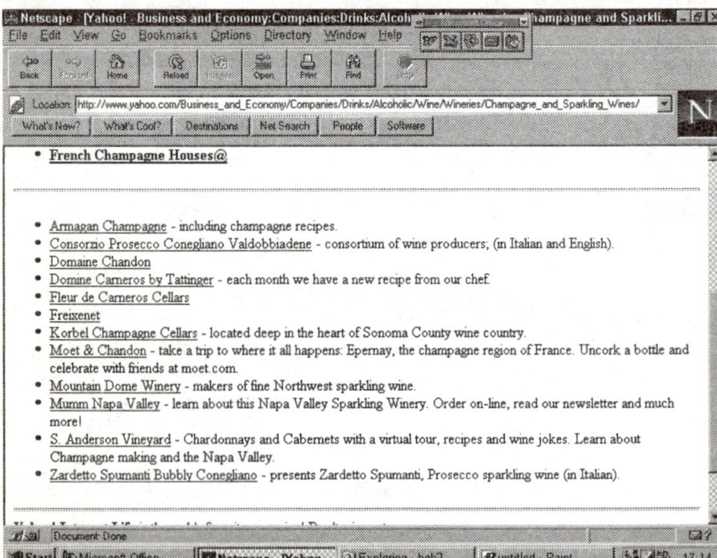

Figure 6.13 A search at Yahoo for sites about Champagne can take you all over the (cyber)world.

AltaVista

AltaVista (http://www.altavista.digital.com) claims to be one of the fastest search engines; it also claims more than 27 million hits every day. It can

(i)

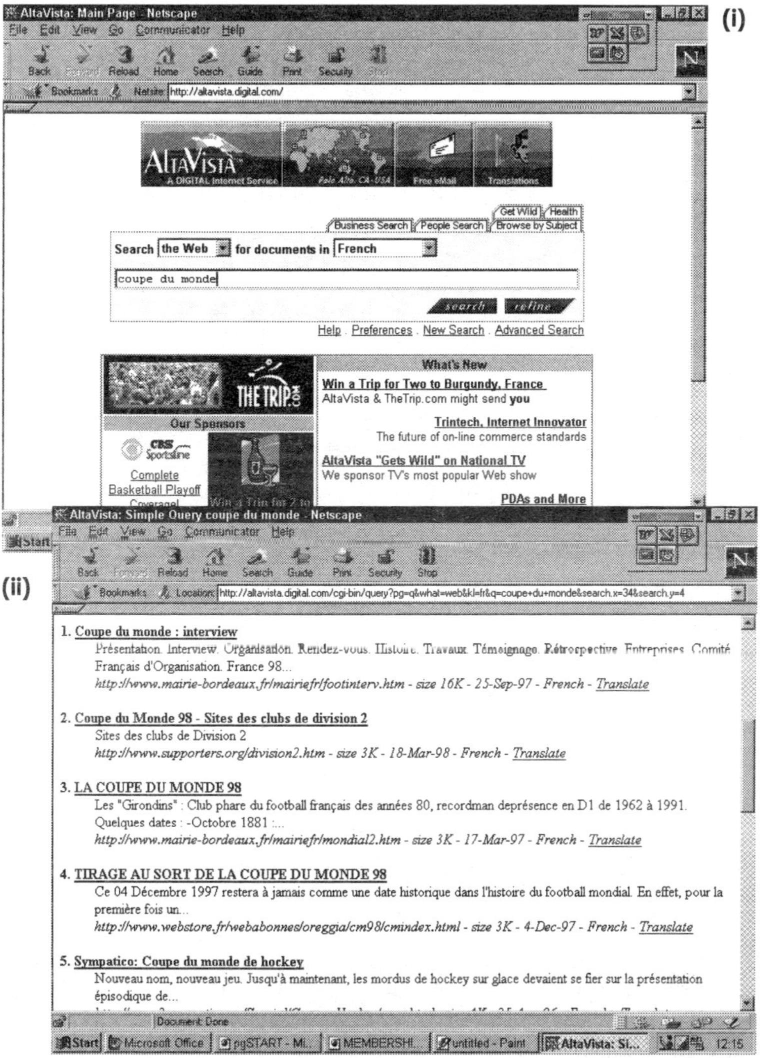

(ii)

Figure 6.14 AltaVista: the language option (i) enables us to look for pages in French, in this case, on the World Cup (ii).

produce an overwhelming amount of information, but does show topics of related interest for you to re-direct your search. AltaVista also enables searching for images.

HotBot

HotBot (http://www.hotbot.com) has a variety of search methods without requiring any special search skills. It allows you to save a profile of search options you would like to run again. It also enables you to narrow your search requirements to specific time periods, for example, just the last week. HotBot, like others, allows you to restrict your search to images.

DejaNews

DejaNews (http://www.dejanews.com) is a specialist search tool for the newsgroups. It tracks about 20,000 groups and is updated several times per day. A search on DejaNews for newsgroup information on, for example, 'Marketing to Children', brings up:

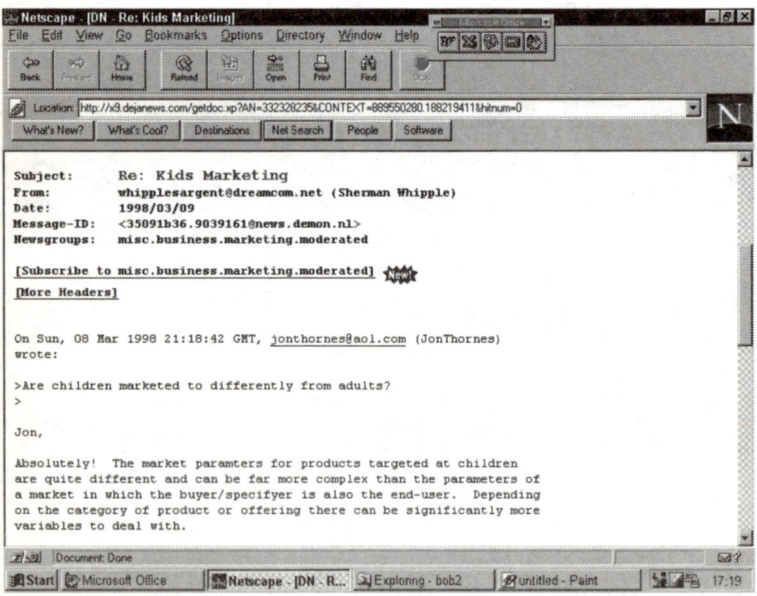

Figure 6.15 DejaNews: for newsgroup conversations, lots of gossip and some gems.

Lycos

Lycos (http://www.lycos.com) enables search refinement and limiting the number of hits. It carries many extras such as city guides and financial news and offers free advertising.

What's New

What's New (http://www.whatsnew.com/whatsnew) is a good place to start when looking for new Web sites. It is also a possible starting-point for identifying new Web-site designs and approaches.

Reference

Reference (http://www.reference.com) tracks e-mail lists and specialist interest groups on the Web.

6.6 Metasearchers

Metasearchers don't carry out your search themselves, but call on other search engines to do the job. This can help if you don't know which search engine to turn to or if you want to search across a mix of potential sources at the same time.

Metacrawler

Metacrawler (http://www.metacrawler.com) accesses the main search engines one at a time and eliminates duplicates.

MetaFind

MetaFind (**http://www.metafind.com**) covers six search engines including AltaVista, Excite, HotBot, and Infoseek. It limits the number of hits from each individual search engine and allows you to fine-tune your search and sort the results by keyword, domain (by country) or alphabetically.

Dogpile

Dogpile (**http://www.dogpile.com**) covers several search engines for the Web but also searches Usenet for newsgroups (via Reference and DejaNews). Dogpile doesn't classify the results, merely lists them by search engine.

Starting Point

Starting Point (**http://www.stpt.com**) embraces several search engines and enables you to try out different ones in turn until you find the most appropriate one. A search to locate information on Champagne in Starting Point, begins:

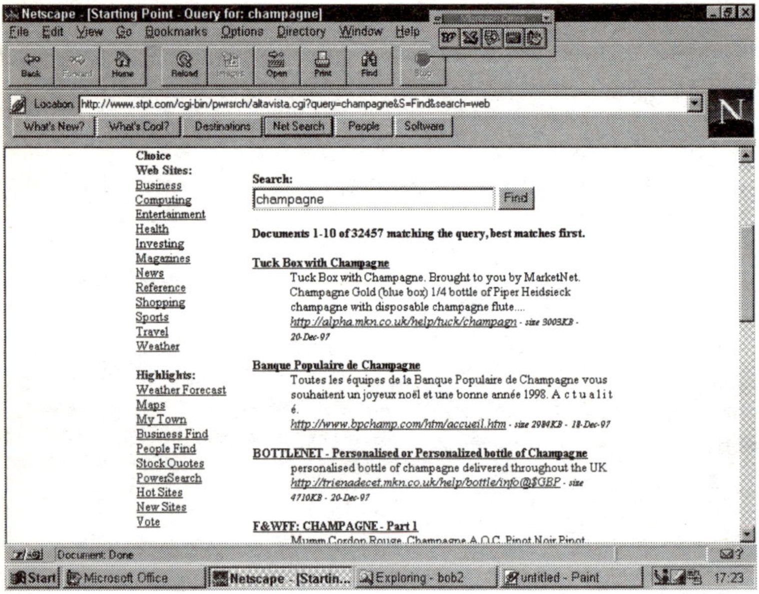

Figure 6.16 Starting Point – like many other search tools – attempts to rank results (hits) by relevance

None of the search engines or metasearchers is truly comprehensive. The amount of information they retrieve, however, still poses problems for someone wanting to pinpoint accurate information fast.

One answer to the problem of information overload is relevance ranking. Here the search engine – and most of them use this approach – evaluates the results according to the number of times your search term is found in the document retrieved.

6.7 Intelligent interfaces

A further search/evaluation tool – an Intelligent Agent – is being devised to perform its search on your behalf while you are fast asleep with the computer switched off. It can identify sites of interest and provide an analysis of those potentially most useful to you and deliver information according to your personalised information needs. The search engine Excite is one such tool which allows you to set up your own profile of requirements and sends the results to your e-mail address. Other Agents learn from you by keeping a record of your previous searches and suggesting new information from the formula of the past.

Some of this may sound 'Brave New World', but it is happening now and improving all the time. One such tool is called **Autonomy** (http://www.agentware.com). At the time of writing, the promise of intelligent interfaces has not been matched by their performance, but like the Web itself, they are still in their infancy and progress is very rapid.

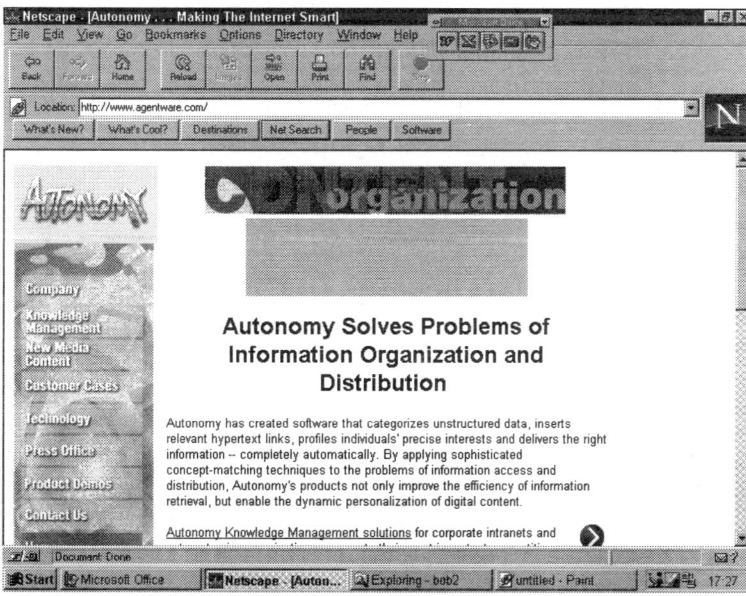

Figure 6.17 Autonomy uses intelligent software to match new information with your requirements and deliver the results to you via e-mail.

6.8 Information overload

If information overload was a problem before the Internet, then its arrival has made the situation worse. When everyone is a publisher and information proliferates on everything how can you tell sound, reliable information from bunkum, especially when you are not knowledgeable about the subject in question?

There is no easy answer but one solution involves adopting some rigorous disciplines towards the access to, and retrieval of, information. At times of pressure, this means restricting your curiosity to the essentials you know you need, instead of exploring that which might be nice to know. It also means:

- Learning the best sources for reliability and accuracy; sticking to the 80–20 rule recognising that 80% of your information comes from about 20% of the places you look for it.
- Verifying, where necessary, sources via e-mail link with colleagues and experts, to distinguish dubious opinion from fact.
- Making use of relevance ranking and trying out intelligent agents.
- Recognising that traditional sources may deliver the information you want more quickly.
- Being ruthless with potential red herrings and keeping your objectives firmly in mind.

6.9 Summary

The World Wide Web is the most widely used feature of the Internet for information searching. It is in a constant state of change and development. It contains trivia you wish to avoid, sites you will find of interest and search tools to locate information of value.

Information overload can get worse with the Web. Personal discipline and sound management practice are even more important when using the vast electronic superstore. Try to identify preferred ways of finding sites of interest in order not to lose too much time in searching or surfing.

Next we illustrate how the Web can be used in business by showing how it can contribute to the development of new products.

7 NEW PRODUCT DEVELOPMENT

7.1 Aims of this chapter

In previous chapters we have indicated how the Internet can help to improve communications, cut costs and facilitate the way business is done by using information resources on a scale hitherto unimaginable. Chapter 7 consolidates what we have covered so far by applying the potential of the Internet to one particular aspect of business – new product development.

Competitive advantage means producing better products and services than the competition at a price the customer is willing to pay. Developing and sustaining competitive advantage invariably requires rapid and reliable information at all stages of the new product development process.

Country-specific business information is growing on the Web, although the majority of the sites on the Web are American in origin. The following outline for new product development concentrates largely on a mix of British and American Web sites.

7.2 The generation of new ideas

Ideas are sometimes generated by concentrated effort but more often by inspiration. Whatever the origins, the creative processes are many and varied. They include scanning newspapers and journals, searching databases of new products, watching what the competition is coming up with, and looking at new market announcements and trade advertising. Now, much of this can be done on the Internet in as systematic or random (surfing) a manner as is appropriate.

The Usenet Newsgroups enable you to seek and test out ideas which are appropriate to that particular group. An alternative to using DejaNews or AltaVista for choosing a newsgroup is the **Experts Exchange** Web site (http://www.experts-exchange.com). This largely focuses on matters related to Information Technology but plans to cast its net wider.

For desk-research, Microsoft **Encarta Concise Encyclopaedia** is free of charge at

http://encarta.msn.com/concise/find/find.asp

The **Electric Library**:

http://www.elibrary.com

and **Encyclopaedia Britannica**:

http://www.eb.com

both make a monthly charge.

The **Internet Public Library**:

http://www.ipl.org

acts as an umbrella site to thousands of others through a subject breakdown which includes the economy, current affairs, geography, quotations, art, biographies and so on.

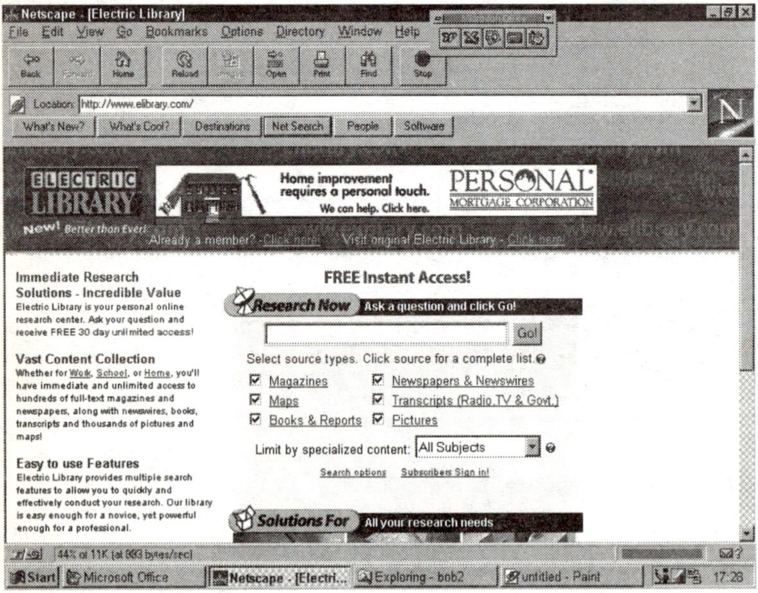

Figure 7.1 The Electric Library: selection from different types of source.

Use the search engines such as Excite and HotBot (see Chapter 6) which tailor information to your needs and feed it to you. A device on HotBot, called **newBot** (http://www.newbot.com) can carry out searches automatically at set times and keep you up to date on your chosen topic.

7.3 Analysing the market

The Web and Usenet are ideally suited to researching market needs and opportunities. Both can provide information about products, companies, markets and customers as well as signals on how markets may change in the future.

One of the primary tools for market analysis on the Internet is sites which specialise in user surveys. The **Graphic, Visualisation and Usability Center** of the Georgia Institute of Technology carries out an annual survey of over 10,000 Web users to gather and analyse information on user and technology demographics, Web and Internet usage, Internet shopping and electronic commerce at

http://www.gvu.gatech.edu/user_surveys

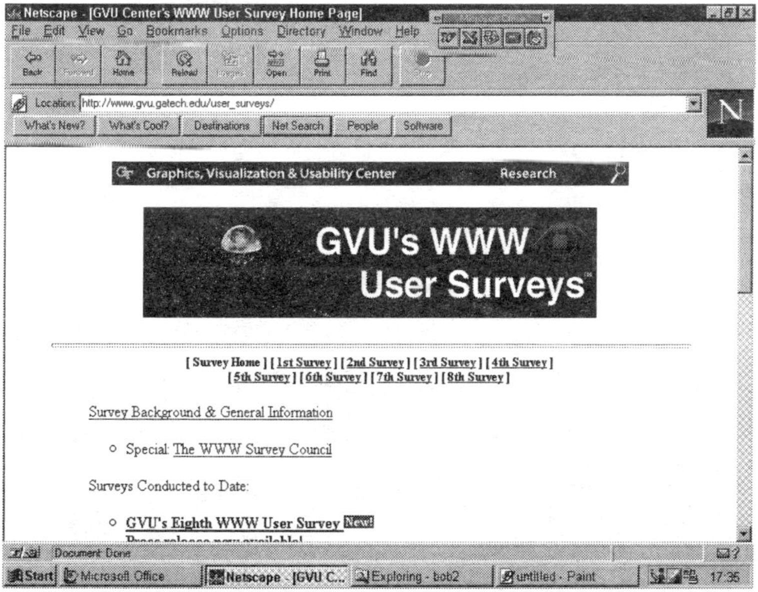

Figure 7.2 GVU offers wide-ranging Internet survey data over 8 years.

We have already mentioned the increasing number of newspaper services that are available on the Web in Chapter 6.

The **NewBot** service mentioned above can keep you in touch with the latest political, cultural and economic news through Wired:

http://www.wired.com

BBC News provides news sections with background and analysis, world coverage by region and business coverage with finance and stockmarket updates:

http://www.bbc.co.uk/news

Dr Ed Yardenni's **Economics Network** has collected together a range of economic statistics and indicators with links to other sites of related interest.

http://www.yardeni.com

IAC InSite provides a Web version of a database which has been around for some time but is continually improving. It offers published information

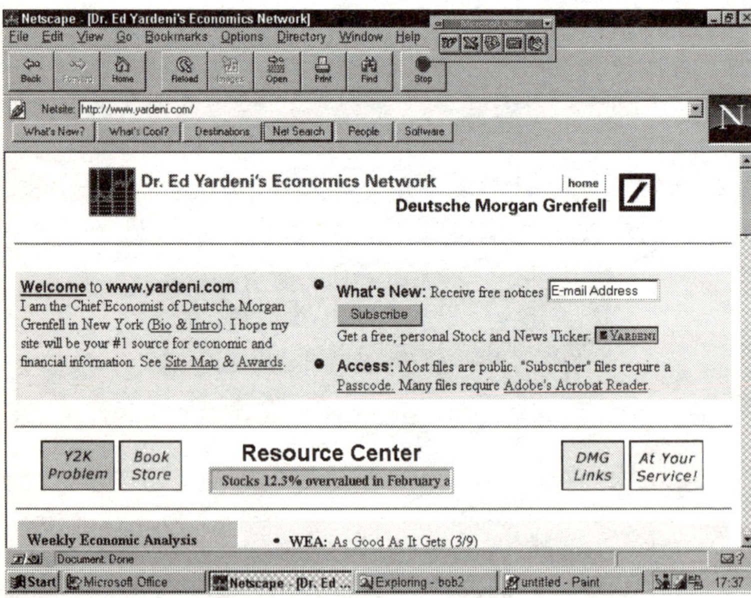

Figure 7.3 Dr Ed Yardenni's Economics Network: Economic analysis and projections from Deutsche Morgan Grenfell.

from journals, newsletters, reports on markets, consumers, and business developments for a flat annual fee.

http://www.iac-insite.com

Don't forget the major search engines (see Chapter 6) where you can search for anything. Another reminder however – too broad a search term will yield an unmanageable number of hits.

7.4 Finding competitors and partners

One of the first things to find out is if another has stolen a march on your idea. If there are several competitors, who is the market leader and how well are they doing? A wealth of industry and company information is available on the Web – on competitors and collaborators as well as on customers and suppliers. There are other collective sources of company information which are growing all the time.

Dun and Bradstreet gives access to details of 17 million companies worldwide and provides mini company reports based on the balance sheet for a small fee per report.

http://www.dunandbrad.co.uk

British Exports Interactive is the Web version of the Kompass British Exports Directory which lets you search 90,000 UK companies by product, service, subject or company name. You have to register for a password before you can view details of the companies. Kompass is expanding to cover many other countries within and outside Europe.

http://www.britishexports.com

Another company initiative is called **Trade UK** which enables you to identify companies by product or service. Again you have to register to see the full company details.

http://www.tradeuk.com

All the **Thomsons business directories** can be found at http://www.inbusiness.co.uk (see Section 6.4) and **Kellys** can be searched at http://www.kellys.reedinfo.co.uk by product or service.

NetPartner's Company Locator can help you find any company's Web site by entering its name, in the following example, Zeneca:

http://www.netpart.com/resource/search.html

(i)

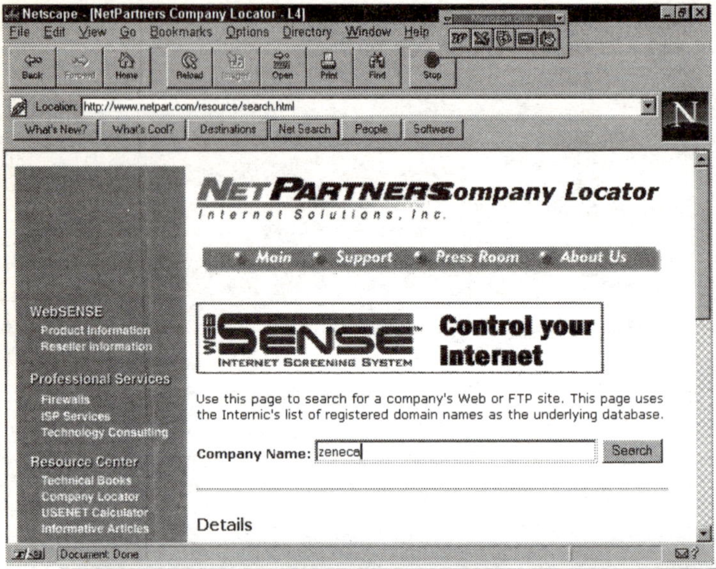

(ii)

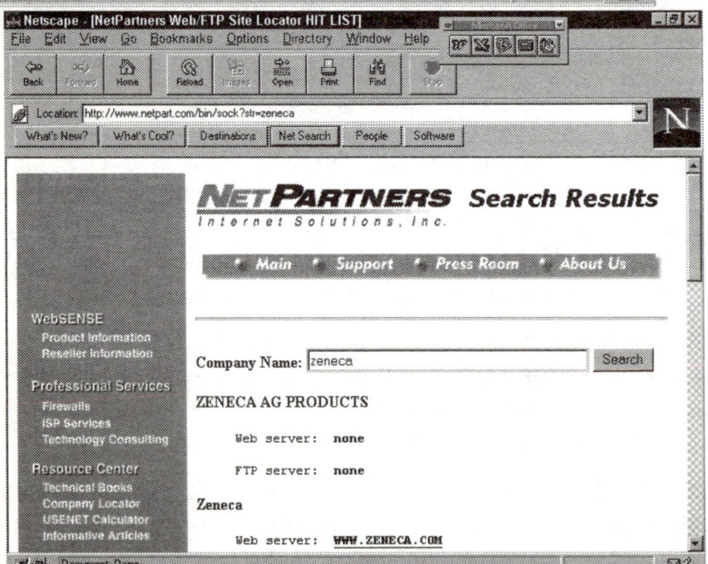

Figure 7.4 Using a Company Name search at NetPartners (i) to locate Zeneca's Web site. A click on *www.zeneca.com* (ii) will now take you there.

Company information has been available online for years through the major commercial vendors. One of these, **Datastar-Dialog**, has collected together an impressive array of databases covering all aspects of business management with details on and leads to companies which are trying out initiatives or exploring new ventures. Datastar-Dialog is now available via the Web as a subscription service at

http://www.dialog.com

A growing number of organisations – public and private sector, service and manufacturing – are building Web sites. Increasingly, these are becoming a primary source for direct information about an organisation's performance and plans. Increasingly too, the Web is becoming a publishing medium for its Annual Report where you can find how well, or badly, it has done over the past year and what its plans are for the next.

7.5 Support and funding

All sorts of information is available on support for business start-up or development. The **Government Information Service** (see Sections 8.3.6 and 8.3.7) has details of regional assistance, grants and loans in its business section.

http://www.open.gov.uk

Business Link National provides advice and support information on a local basis throughout the UK including details of grants and subsidies.

http://www.businesslink.co.uk

The **Business Bureau (UK)** is a source of information on many aspects of business and easy to navigate.

http://www.u-net.com/bureau

Business Credit Management sources information on company finance, major banks and financial forecasts.

http://www.creditman.co.uk

There are also sites which provide free legal information for companies such as **The Legal Resources** pages

http://www.pavilion.co.uk/legal/welcome.htm

or the **Legal 500**

http://www.icclaw.com

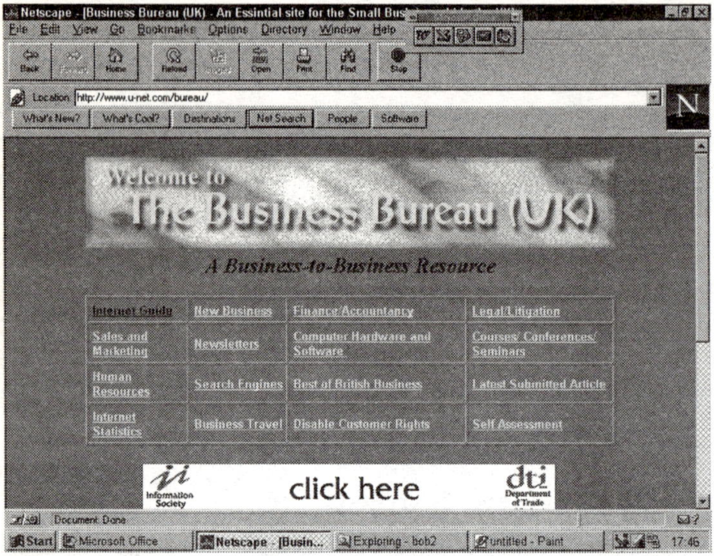

Figure 7.5 The Business Bureau: focus on information for businesses.

Figure 7.6 **ICC Law: recommended firms and legal information covering the UK, Europe and Asia/Pacific.**

7.6 Research and development

In the past, as a product or service traditionally went through the stages of R&D, design, testing and on to production, the development phases have been relatively discrete and sequential, with each phase being signed off before the next is tackled. One of the potentially valuable aspects of the Internet as a business medium is that it is interactive, enabling actual and potential customers to be kept constantly in touch about developments. One of the benefits of this live to-and-fro of information between producer and consumer is that formerly sequential processes requiring long lead-in times can be integrated into a continuing process, helping to keep the product or service flexible, and shortening the time between design and delivery.

The customer is not always right and this can be irksome. But closeness to customers is a vital ingredient of competitive advantage and this interactivity can bring enormous rewards.

Let us take the example of a new all-singing, all-dancing widget, the core elements of which have been more or less decided so that the production process can start up. If the organisation's Web site is used to depict the design in process, the product becomes more customer-driven as it develops. This process can take place while technical problems are being researched for solutions with newsgroups and scientific, technical and engineering databases.

Most search engines have a specialist scientific/technical/ engineering domain. One useful starting point might be the scientific site Keysites, run by the editors of the **New Scientist Magazine** (http://www.keysites.com). This has a Hot Spots section which provides current overviews of hundreds of scientific sites on the Web.

Customer feedback during the testing and design stages can help avoid serious errors and lead to modifications being made while they are still manageable. Feedback can be obtained from specified customers who are assigned a password, or from all and sundry as required. Alternatively, you can use one of the mailing lists available from sites such as:

Liszt which has over 70,000 indexed mailing lists:

http://www.liszt.com

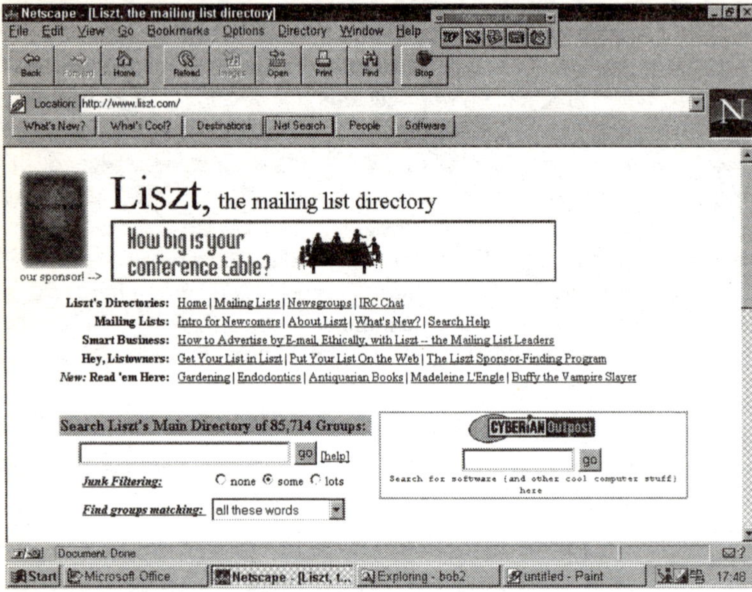

Figure 7.7 Liszt: an indexed search to mailing lists on hundreds of topics and sectors.

Publicly Accessible Mailing Lists:

http://www.neosoft.com/internet/paml

The list of lists, available at

http://www.catalog.com/vivian/interest-group-search.html

7.7 Advertising and promotion

Product or service promotion is one of the main uses of the Web, which has been described as one huge shopping precinct. With no distribution costs, ease and speed of updating and modification, and a potential market of millions of consumers, the Web is ideally suited to advertising and promotion.

You have to take care, however, to be aware of the pitfalls of the new medium. You may produce a marketing brochure once every year or two; such practice is inadequate for the Web, whose visitors constantly require something new, something to grab their interest and something to get involved in so they will want to return. We shall look at the implications of setting up a Web site in Chapter 8 and at advertising possibilities in Section 8.3.12.

In the meantime, as you move from site to site on the Web, make a mental note of (and perhaps, add to your list of Bookmarks or Favorites) what you find appealing, or boring, that which you might make use of by adapting it to your needs, or that which you would not wish to see again!

7.8 Distribution

The fundamental difference between the traditional forms of distribution and the Internet is that on the Internet the customer comes to you.

The Internet can change the way products can be delivered, especially those which are information-based, such as books, newspapers, magazines, or anything involving a mix of text, sound or pictures. Such products can be downloaded from the Web at much lower costs than those of traditional print and distribution. This has great advantages for distribution, but significant implications for copyright and ownership which we look at in Chapters 9 and 10.

In the case of goods which cannot be physically delivered over the Internet, many company Web sites now enable you to leave your enquiry or specific order by constructing forms for you to complete. You then e mail the form for processing by the company which would contact you via traditional – terrestial – means for following up the enquiry or delivering the goods.

More on buying and selling on the Web in Chapter 9.

7.9 Managing operations

Managing operations is an all-embracing term designed to cover those everyday procedures involved in keeping the business ticking over. Whatever the day to day routine, it is traditionally characterised by increasing quantities of paperwork.

Recruitment practices, for example, can be re-invented on the Web where notice of a job vacancy can reach a wider audience at home and abroad at a fraction of the cost of its printed and circulated predecessor. Look back to Chapter 6 for examples of recruitment sites.

Recruitment can be complemented by use of personality or IQ tests available through sites such as the following:

Management Development provides links to a number of tests:

http://www.pikeperry.co.uk/ppp/md/person.htm

Personality and IQ Tests provides tests on self-awareness including some humorous ones, and feeds back results auto-matically. It is up to you how much trust you place in such tools!

http://www.davideck.com/

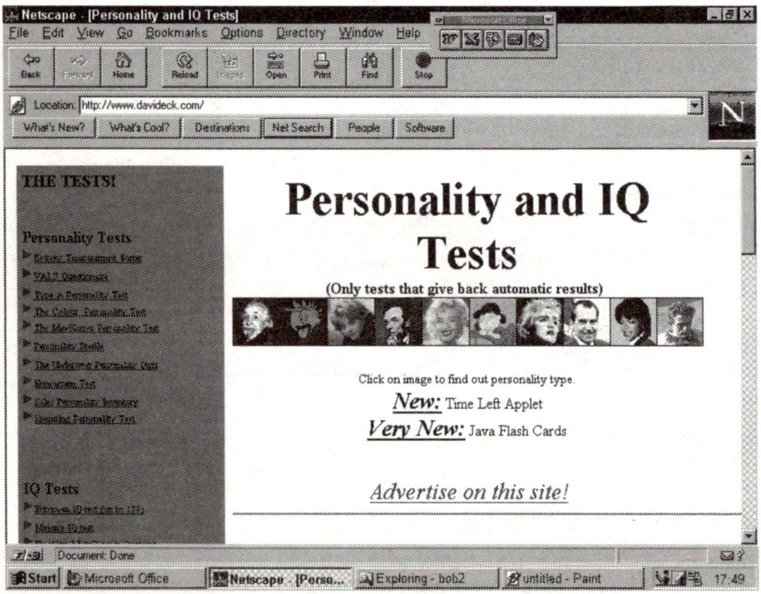

Figure 7.8 Personality and IQ tests: one mouse-click to discover the personality behind the face.

With more companies using the Internet to promote their products and services, it offers an alternative way of identifying and comparing new suppliers. Purchasers can use the Web to place invitations to tender for new orders or services.

Organisational messaging and communication systems, whatever the distance involved, can not only reduce storage and distribution costs by using e-mail, but also improve speed and flexibility. With the data in electronic form, it can be adapted and re-used or passed on to others for action.

7.10 Training and development

Management training and development does not come just at the end of the new product development life-cycle. Increasingly it is recognised that professional development is a continuing process throughout your career. There are a number of Web sites designed to offer support with this:

The European Case Clearing House has a comprehensive bibliography with abstracts of over 14,000 management teaching cases from business schools around the world.

http://www.ecch.cranfield.ac.uk

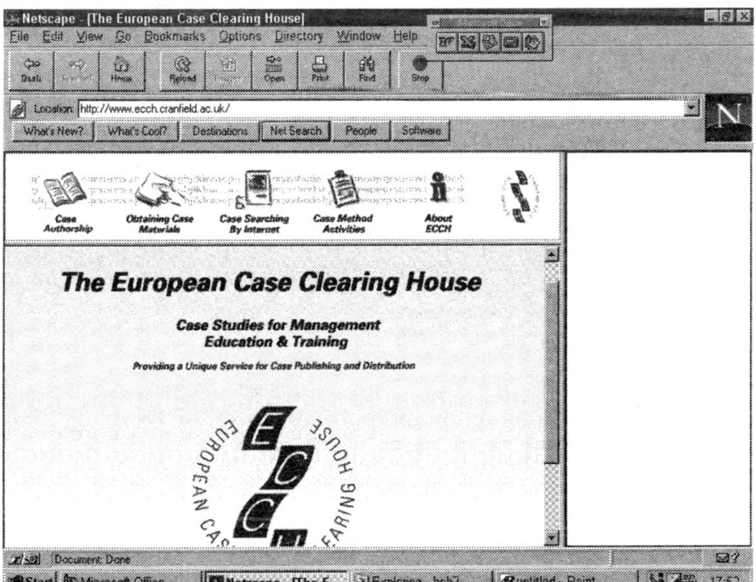

Figure 7.9 The ECCH collects teaching cases from major business schools including Harvard, INSEAD and IMD.

The Institute of Management is developing a site covering all aspects of management development with links to sites of related interest (see Section 8.3.9).

http://www.inst-mgt.org.uk

FT Mastering Management provides regularly updated case studies from recent editions of the FT that bring the latest management concepts to life.

http://www.ftmastering.com

Business Management and Technology Research provides a map of contemporary business, management and IT issues with access to many other sources and hundreds of full-text articles and papers.

http://www.brint.com

The **WWW Project Management Forum** is a non-profit resource for information on all kinds of international project management affairs.

http://www.pmforum.org

The **Management Archive** is the Web site of the Academy of Management which provides a forum for management ideas, conferences, research, working papers and discussion lists.

http://ursus.jun.alaska.edu

7.11 Summary

With its capability of contributing to all phases of new product development, from the initial idea through design to point of sale, the Internet is now convincing even the most sceptical that it is beginning to turn into a significant business tool for the future.

Further evidence of it potential will be brought out in the next two chapters where we look at designing a Web site and consider buying and selling on the Web.

8 DESIGNING A WEB SITE

8.1 Aims of this chapter

Now that you have had an opportunity to look at some Web sites and pick up one or two ideas on what they can do, we are going to consider how to build one of your own. This involves putting strategy and marketing at the forefront of our thinking. It is timely, therefore, to reflect on the kind of questions we asked at the end of Chapter 2:

What are we really trying to achieve?

How can the Internet improve the way we do things?

What level of investment are we prepared to commit?

8.2 Marketing on the Web

So what is different about the World Wide Web and what are its most important features?

It may not be harder to target particular groups than it is through conventional advertising, but you have to start thinking about it in different ways. Electronic consumers have more choice and more control over what they choose to see than television viewers or newspaper readers. Newsgroup subscribers can pick which messages they like and ignore the rest. You cannot tell who has read your message unless they let you know. On the World Wide Web, the provider is essentially passive waiting for the consumer to choose where they visit, when and for how long. As with any other media, however, there are ways and means of finding out who has seen your marketing message (see Section 10.6). This information enables you to become more proactive and creative by slanting the content of your site towards those who visit it most, or towards those whom you wish to attract.

As it is the user who chooses to look at the information, the necessity to make it interesting and attractive is even more important than for TV or hard-copy advertising. Just as in the real world, Internet users have many claims on their attention and are becoming increasingly sophisticated and demanding.

There are very few restrictions on the amount of information you can make available and the formats you use. You can choose text, colour, graphics, even sound and video. Remember, however, that some customers may not be able to take advantage of these features: they may not, for example, have speakers to hear sound, or may prefer to 'switch off' the images on a feature on their browser. In addition, the more you do, the more it costs in terms of design, disk-space and the amount of time you spend updating and changing the information.

There are no barriers of time and space. The Internet does not close; it is open 24 hours a day, 7 days a week. The Web is world-wide. Hence your site is as likely to receive visitors from the other side of the world as it is from the next town. This offers a wonderful potential for new customers, but it also creates dangers for the unaware. While the Internet has boosted the use of English as the language of business, the need to take account of cultural sensitivities and differences is as acute on the Web as it is in everyday life. Foreign language advertisements, however, can imply deliberately targeted marketing and this can imply liability in those foreign markets. We shall look at this closer in Chapter 10.

Electronic communications are interactive. There are various ways for a visitor to a Web site to send a message, reply to a question, or take part in an activity. These conversations offer both threats and opportunities to the marketer. If you make claims that are untrue, insensitive or just plain stupid, then hundreds of thousands of potential consumers can know about it in minutes via e-mail and newsgroups. An upset customer can all too easily pass on notices of dissatisfaction. On the other hand, the potential for building relationships with customers takes on a different dimension on the Web where suppliers can easily learn of customer attitudes. This potential must be developed through creating opportunities for interactivity and making them interesting to the visitor.

The Internet enables a London cabbie to stand side by side with IBM in the marketplace. It is as easy – often easier – for a small firm or an individual to set up a Web site as it is for a multinational. Although the larger organisation will have more resources than the smaller, the latter is often quicker to respond and adapt than those encumbered by decision-making hierarchies and bureaucracies. A couple of pages are within the reach of everyone as a limited amount of space on the Web is usually provided free of charge by the Internet Access Provider as part of your subscription. Everyone is encouraged to be a publisher on the Web.

As market entry is low-cost on the Web, it increases the need for businesses to track what others are doing and to keep up with new developments on the Web itself. As technologies evolve they are impacting on the very nature of marketing itself. We look at some implications for the future in Chapter 14.

8.3 12 steps to creating a Web site

1 Ask yourself why you are bothering

Consider what it is that you want to achieve. Is your Web site going to be:

- A way of attracting new customers?
- An experiment to see what return you get?
- A public relations statement?
- An effort to keep up with the Joneses?
- A vehicle for providing a service?
- A replacement for – or alternative to – product information handbooks?
- For fun – many others are!

This is the time to ask what benefits you expect from a Web site bearing in mind how much time, money and technical and human resource you are going to invest in it.

It is also the time to reflect on how you will measure success. Quantifying the cost-benefits of marketing can be difficult at the best of times. On the Web you will need to consider trapping information about who visits your site and what they look at, or do when they get there.

This first process is a vital one and should be linked to your overall business strategy. We will take a closer look at developing an Internet strategy in Chapter 12.

2 Keep up-to-date with how audience profiles are changing on the Web

Strategy and objectives are closely linked to customers – or target audience. We looked at growth figures and some broad profiles in Chapters 1 and 2. But the Internet is moving so fast that current surveys are the only really valid ones – if you can trust them!

Although traditional marketing requirements and skills still apply, there is now an even greater emphasis on creativity. It is important not to design a site blinkered by the thinking and the restrictions of the past.

3. Find an organisation to host your Web site

Renting space on a computer run by an Internet Access Provider has become an established method of setting up on the Web.

Most Internet Access Providers offer some free disk space – usually about 5–10 Mb as part of their package. This is often sufficient for starting up and experimenting, providing the cheapest and lowest-risk option. You must, of course, identify the right Internet Access Provider (Chapter 4). Remember to ask questions concerning developments for your site.

- Who looks after the updating?
- What kind of information can I get about site usage?
- Are there any restrictions on the type of software that the host will accept on their server?
- Can I buy more space? How much will it cost?

External design consultants will also usually host your site but the quid pro quo is that you buy their design services.

Large organisations may host their Web sites on their own server. This requires a significant investment in hardware and software and considerable technical knowledge and skill.

4 Decide whether you are going to build your Web site in-house or outsource it

Having chosen where you are going to host the site, you need to consider who is going to design it.

Outsourcing should provide you with a professional site which can then be brought back in-house for updating and maintaining. Think about whether you want to update and maintain it yourself or hand that over too.

Remember that outsourcing does not absolve you from responsibility and effort. Apart from the costs involved, it will entail large amounts of time spent in explaining the business to the outside agency. No one ever knows your business as well as you.

In-house development may be more, or less, costly depending on whether you bring in specialist staff, or on how you cost the time of existing staff which is spent in learning and development.

There are thousands of Web site designers: good ones and not so good ones. Your Internet Access Provider, or other contacts may be able to recommend a designer, or you will find plenty available at the **Brit Index**:

http://www.yacc.co.uk/britind/internet.html

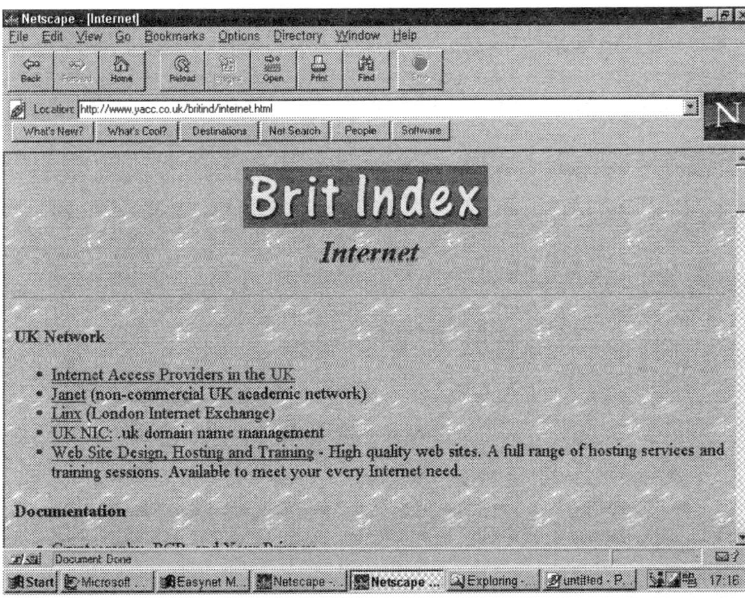

Figure 8.1 The Brit Index: information on Web site designers, trainers, hosting services and access providers.

As a general rule, you should ask the same questions as when you take on any external consultant:

- What work have they already accomplished? Ask to see some examples and some references from other clients.

- What work has been done for companies like yours, how successful was it, and how was success measured?
- How can the designer demonstrate their capability of working to deadlines and within agreed costs?
- Who will actually do the work? Is it the person you are talking to or will it be a back-room boffin whose natural language is techno-babble?
- Obtain more than one estimate and ask around to find out what fees might be usual for this kind of work.

5 Register your domain name

Your domain name is similar to your URL (Uniform Resource Locator) and consists of your company name and codes for the organization type and country of origin. On the Web, it is – like your company name – one of the first things by which people identify you and what you do. Your domain name is one of the main ways by which people will find you on the Web. (Look back to Section 6.3 for an explanation of URLs). It needs to be registered before you can use it.

Figure 8.2 Nominet: for registering a domain name in the UK

The easiest way to register your domain name is via your Internet Access Provider and there is usually a charge of between £100 and £200.

- In the UK domain names are registered with an organisation called **Nominet** (http://www.nic.uk).
- In the USA the registration organisation is **Internic** (http://www.internic.net).

These bodies can provide interesting suggestions for names along with various rules and guidance. Choose a domain name that reflects your usual business or trading name. Don't be too disappointed if your first choice has already been used – millions of domain names have already been registered. There have been cases of Web domain names being challenged by organisations who consider their brand name has been 'stolen' by another. Such claims are being supported in courts of law. There are sites where you can check to see if a name has already been registered

http://rs.internic.net/cgi-bin/whois

or

http://www.pipex.net/~guyd/name-chk.html).

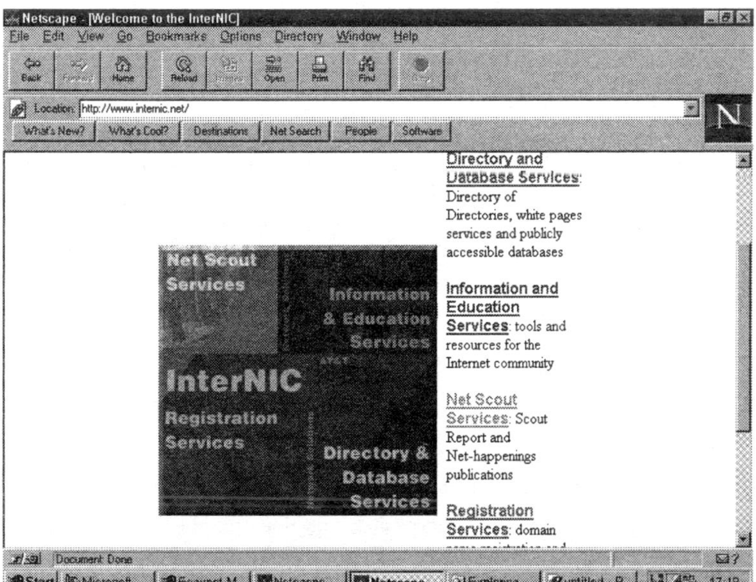

Figure 8.3 Internic: for registering a domain name in the USA

6 Think carefully about the construction of your site

The first page of your site, referred to as the Home Page is your first welcome to visitors. You should, by now, have seen quite a few, and be able to pick out aspects of Web sites that you like and don't like. When constructing your own site you need to:

- Be clear about what you want to achieve otherwise you will confuse your visitors.
- Think about issues of design – how will the image you wish to convey be reflected?
- Consider how you can entice visitors deeper into the site.
- Think of navigation around the site – how many mouse-clicks will it take to find something of interest? Can you short-circuit the process?
- Reflect the different aspects of your company and the importance you attach them.

You will need to ask for the opinions of potential users here. Their view of a helpful layout may differ from yours.

FRAMES

One popular way of improving navigation around a site and reducing the number of mouse clicks is the use of Frames. This splits the screen into two as in Figure 8.4. The left-hand side of the screen with the site menu is static while the right-hand side changes according to the choices you make. Some older browsers cannot read frames so some sites are made available in two versions – with and without frames.

7 Consider the content of the site

Consideration has to be given to whether information is:

- one-way (pull) – to the potential customer for them to pull from the information-base you have made available
- one-way (push) – targeted and e-mailed to specific individuals or groups
- two-way – interactive so that you enter into a dialogue with the visitor/customer through e-mail or Chat

(i)

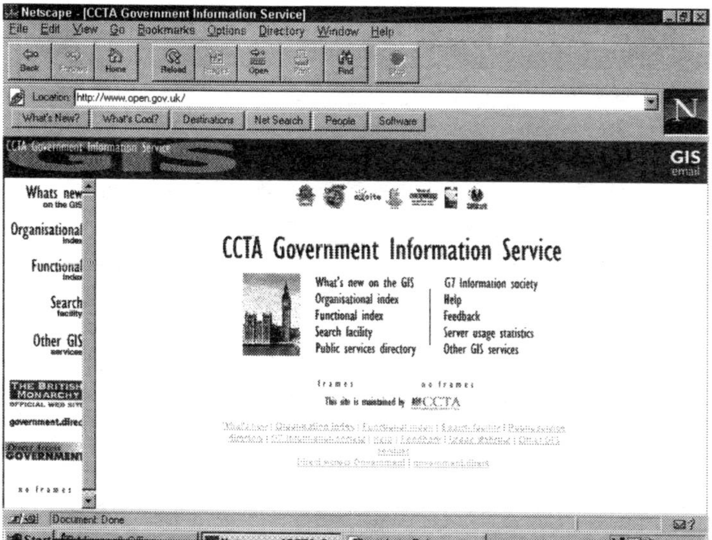

(ii)

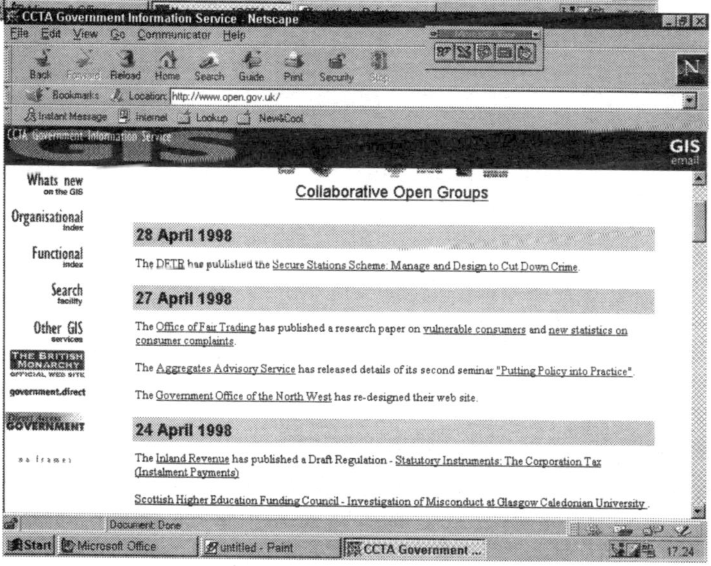

Figure 8.4 Frames in use at at GIS: a click on What's New (i) takes us to some current affairs options (ii) from which we select statistics about consumer complaints (iii). The Frames on the left stay with us throughout, enabling rapid navigation to other parts of the site.

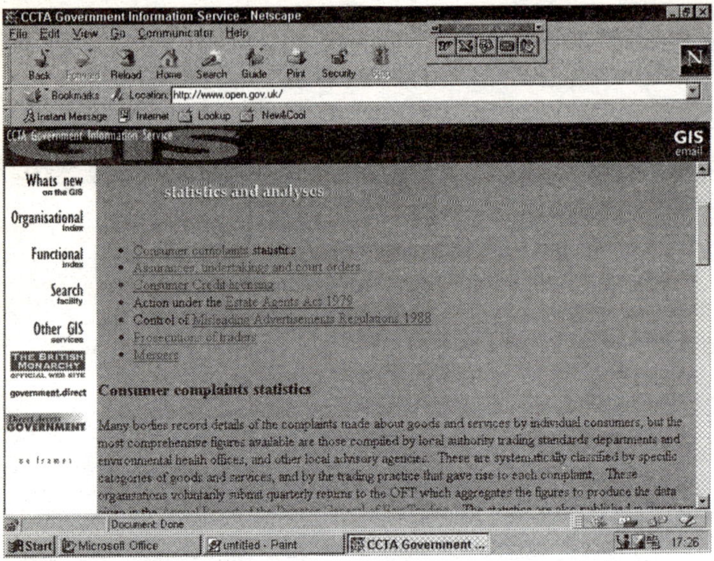

(iii)

- multi-way – information is broadcast, shared, and re-collected on a wide platform where customers can interact with other customers as well as directly with the organisation. Web sites are increasingly used for this kind of activity as well as newsgroups.

Think about:

- The various problems and complaints your customers have and how the Web can help to resolve them.
- Adding value on the Web by making available those snippets of information your customers value on a regular basis, and will come back for time and again.
- Making it desirable for the customer to return. Learn about customer preferences, but do remember that if you want the customer to disclose private or confidential information about themselves, then it has to be worth their while.

The quality of experience your site offers to visitors and building trust and reliability. If the Web appears to be a daunting black hole, then they will quickly go elsewhere.

VIRTUAL REALITY

Some retailers are exploring Virtual Reality on the Web to make the shopping experience as 'real' from the desktop as it is in the supermarket.

Virtual Reality hit popular consciousness by bringing a 3-D reality to children's screen games. It was also popularised in the book (and film) *Disclosure* by Michael Crichton. It is no longer the stuff of science fiction. It is only its ravenous appetite for huge amounts of computer memory – and the availability of broadband cables – which is slowing its progress and applications on the Internet.

Already, a number of retailers – especially supermarkets wishing to make home-shopping a 'real' experience – are exploring the potential to see if you can (virtually) pick a book from the shelves, put shopping in your trolley, try on a pair of shoes, be at holiday locations, or test-drive a new car.

8 Use colour, video and graphics

We have already mentioned that colour, graphics and especially video take time to come through the telephone lines. Although a moderate use of them can greatly enhance the attractiveness of your site, they can also render your site difficult and time-consuming to use. Whereas large organisations may have ISDN or a leased line to speed up access and delivery, most home users will be using modems, which are much slower.

Some designers argue that the classical design rules still apply on the Web:

- Use black, red and white as the major colours.
- Use different font-sizes to indicate points or thoughts you wish to emphasise.
- Avoid text which is too tiny to read without a magnifying glass.

Although the cost of disc space is very low in cyberspace, information overload is already a problem. Think of how you like to read and absorb new information, perhaps with plenty of white space on the page/screen, in clear, concise and simple-to-understand language. Keep things brief and to-the-point with no long, rambling sentences. Don't be like some web site producers who think that quantity – not quality – is the key.

9 Plan related hyperlinks and gateways

Hyperlinks will of course form the foundation of your site with links from one document to another. You also need, however, to point users to other sites which might be of interest to them. These will usually be sites that give more information on a particular topic or cover a complementary activity to which you may want to refer. Below we show some sample selection criteria, in this case from the Institute of Management, which is setting up links to external business and management sites.

The Institute of Management
Management Directory Selection Criteria

Information Content

Relevance: link sites focus on the theory and practice of management.

Objectivity: any bias is declared; the site contains information over and above product or service marketing.

Accuracy: the information (as far as can be determined) is accurate and up-to-date.

Authority: the originator of the Web site is in a position to lend authority to the information presented.

Depth: topics are more than superficial or personal opinion and are treated in reasonable depth.

Ease of Access

Access to the site is unrestricted. If the site (or part of it) is password-controlled, or open only to subscribers, it should still meet the criteria above.

Ease of Use

The site is well laid out and easy to navigate. If relevant, there is an online facility for joining or ordering and it is possible to e-mail the originating organisation from the site.

Site Stability

The site URL is stable, or good pointers are made if changes affecting access and content are made.

Figure 8.5 Institute of Management: organising access to different types – and sites – of information about management. The Management Link (i) splits into Management Skills and Management Sources.

(iii)

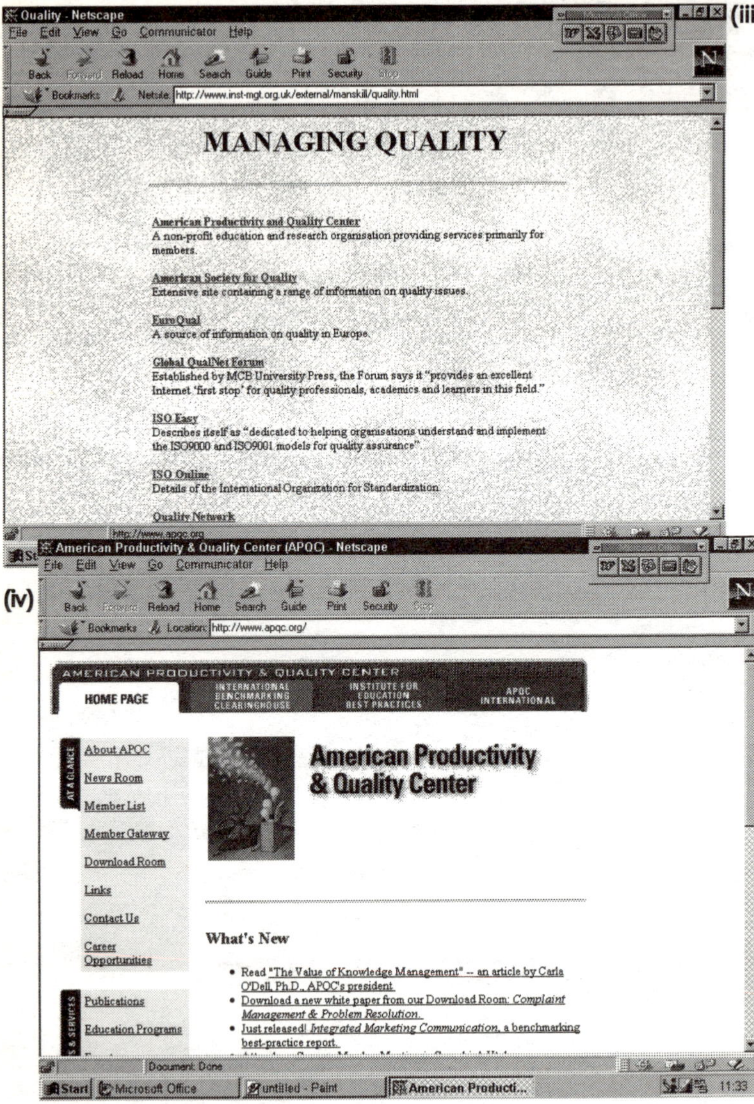

(iv)

Clicking on Management Skills, in search of some recent American skills initiatives, finds Quality as a major signpost (ii). A click on Quality brings up a menu of further options (iii), the first of which is for the American Productivity and Quality Center (iv).

10 Strive for interactivity and involvement

A successful Web site means encouraging your visitors to participate and get involved. There are a number of ways to do this, for example: by getting them to offer comments, suggestions or criticisms; take part in product design or testing; get involved in quizzes, tests or imaginatively constructed games which are meaningful to your customers and your products.

Remember that anything more than straight e-mail replies requires fairly sophisticated design and programming. It is worthwhile, however, making your site attention-grabbing and attractive to come back to.

Remember, if you encourage people to ask questions and make suggestions, do not forget to respond to, and deal with, enquiries.

STAFF TRAINING IN HTML

Don't forget staff training. Even if your site is set up and run by an external third party, it will be beneficial to the organisation for staff to be able to understand and design their own text and hyperlinks for the Web. Hyper Text Markup Language (HTML) is not difficult to learn – Teach Yourself HTML will soon show you how to produce an effective and attractive Web site.. Microsoft Word 7 also 'translates' to the HTML format and packages such as Microsoft's FrontPage and Claris' HomePage makes the job easier.

11 Consider security issues

Unless you protect it, information that you put on the Web is for public consumption by a worldwide market. It is virtually impossible to follow and police what might happen to your information once it is downloaded to any of the 60+ million computers linked up, notwithstanding international laws on copyright (see Chapter 10).

If there are sections of your Web site that you would wish to secure for some categories of user or customer only, then form a closed user group to which only password-holders are allowed access.

If you wish your Web site to link to more sensitive information to which access must be even more strictly controlled, for example your customer database, then it is becoming standard practice to protect such information from abuse or misuse with a firewall. (A firewall is another computer through which all access traffic is routed, vetted and strictly controlled. Anything that does not meet access criteria can be shut out.)

12 Promote the site

Unless people know your address – your URL – they will find you in one of a number of ways:

- They will visit your site as a result of a hypertext link from another
- They will use one of the search engines to find you
- Word of mouth recommendation
- They will have seen some of your advertising
- It will be by chance.

It is important that the search engines pick up your site. Your Home Page is the one that search engines will use for indexing your site and therefore it needs to contain the important concepts and terms that people may use to find you. These may be apparent to the user or hidden away where only the search engines will find them. Although English is the first language of the Web, if you are targeting a particular country, think of their language – if France is your goal, for example, then use French.

The Internet can facilitate advertising to as generic or specific a target audience as required. With e-mail enabling the consumer to respond immediately, the advertiser has to think differently from press or TV advertising. Advertising is following a number of patterns or models on the Web:

1 **Banners**: small rectangular graphics like roadside billboards appearing on popular consumer sites. Once static, they are becoming increasingly animated and interactive.
2 **Buttons**: similar to banners, but usually contain a corporate name, or the brand, or even the industry. A click on the button will take you to that company's corporate Web site. At the bottom of the Electronic Library's Home Page (see Section 7.2) are a number of buttons – a click on Tandem, for example, takes you straight there.
3 **Co-branded sponsorships**: here the attempt is to get users to identify with the mission of the site by integrating products and brands with the editorial content.

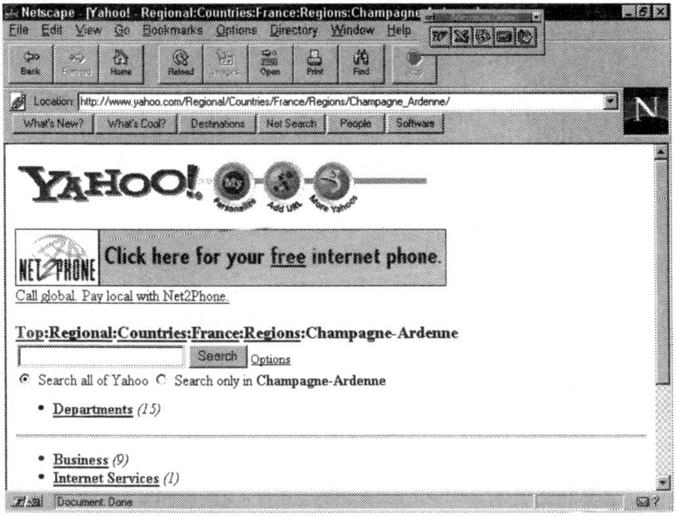

Figure 8.6 A banner advertisement for Net Phones. See the Internet Movie Database (page 64) or the Electric Library (page 76) for others.

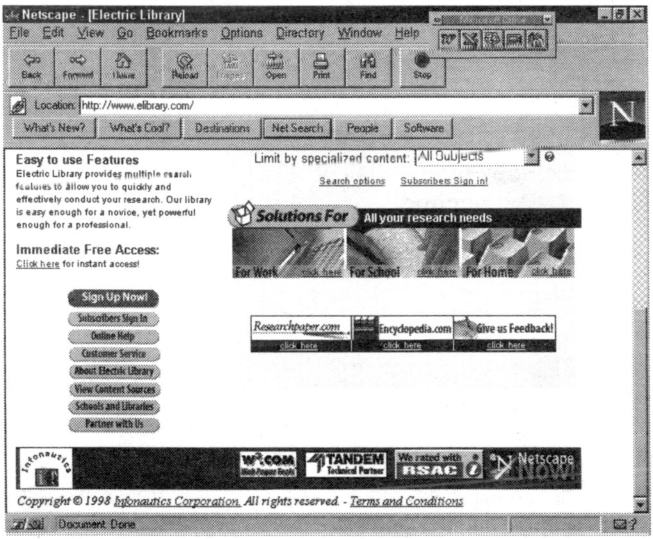

Figure 8.7 The four button ads at the bottom of this page provide one-click access to the sites which paid for them.

4. **Keywords**: here advertisers can 'buy' a term! For example, if Adidas were to buy the term 'football boots', any time someone does a search for 'football boots' on a particular search engine, the name Adidas will pop up on the screen. Here, we pursue our interest in Champagne.

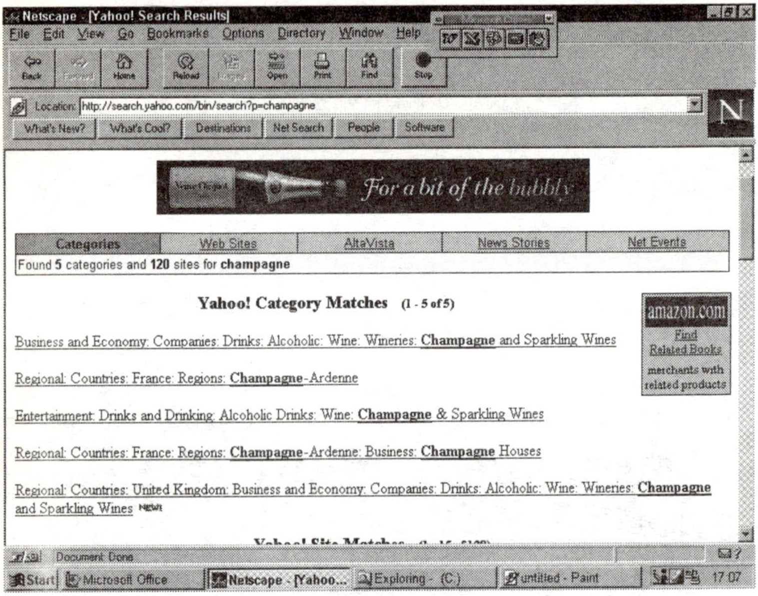

Figure 8.8 The image of the bottle of bubbly was activated by entering the keyword 'Champagne'.

Look back to Chapter 6 for other examples of Button, Banner and Keyword advertising.

Your Web site will also need promotion through more traditional media such as business cards, marketing literature, company reports or press or media campaigns. Remember though that the Web is about marketing, so be wary about using one marketing medium to market another. The real trick to a successful Web site is not how much you promote it but in the value that visitors/customers can derive from it. It will then promote itself.

8.4 Some costs to consider

- The amount of space you buy (from the Internet Access provider) for your Web site, usually quoted in megabytes, but translatable into pages. Alternatively, the costs of running your own server (look back to Section 4.3).
- The amount of development work needed for your site. Small sites can be easy to put up and are cheap. More sophisticated sites featuring various design elements and perhaps using commercial transaction software (see next chapter) can run into tens of thousands of pounds.
- The amount of time you will need to spend updating and modifying the site, and the training you – or your staff – will need to undergo in order to be competent to do this. People-time is the usually the biggest cost of all and difficult to estimate with accuracy.

  You may need to bring in an experienced Webmaster.

WEBMASTER

A Webmaster is responsible for the design, development and maintenance of a site in both the technical and content aspects. This requires a rare combination of IT, information, design and interpersonal skills.

- The cost of promotion through traditional, as well as electronic, means.

It is important not to expect profit of any kind straightaway. It will take time to find your way around and learn from mistakes. It is much better that you define the project as a current cost-centre and as an investment for the future.

8.5 Summary

- Investigate the Web as a communication and marketing medium.
- Assess your current resources, especially people skills.
- Assess the fit of your products/services with the Web for

your customers.

- Determine what you want from the Web site, the benefits to your organisation and how you will measure success.
- Determine the key benefits and value that the customer will derive from the site.
- Get support from other parts of the organisation and assign a pilot approach to a project manager or Webmaster.
- Remember that the Web has its own marketing conventions.
- Decide if you need to call in an external designer, but don't

9 BUYING AND SELLING ON THE WEB

9.1 Aims of this chapter

The Web has been projected as the income-generation medium of the new millennium. There have been early successes, although, in the main, these have been software companies which have made money out of the Web, rather than on the Web. There are promising signs from other sectors, however, where some companies are beginning to make money, and others – if not making money directly – are making it indirectly through leads that would probably not have been generated without the Web.

So just how feasible is buying and selling on the Internet? What are the issues to be aware of?

The key questions are:

- What do you have to sell and how suited is it to the Internet?
- How do you make payments on the Internet?
- What guarantees of security and confidentiality do the technologies offer the customer?

9.2 Forecasts

Towards the end of his first term in office, Bill Clinton pronounced that cyberspace (the Internet) was going to turn into 'a global free-trade zone' which would provide 'a safe and stable terrain' for people to do business. We have summarised the main points of these White House proposals at the end of Chapter 10. The US President was able to make such proposals against the background of forecasts, one of which put Internet turnover at some $1 trillion by the year 2010. Another contemporary survey by the consultancy KPMG revealed that large British companies expected 35% of all sales to be handled over the Internet by the year 2002, equivalent to about £350 billion in turnover.

Other forecasts have been less ambitious, but all agree that by the year 2000, the Internet will be the vehicle for anything from $20 billion to $200 billion in gross turnover.

9.3 The current reality

Moves towards sales on the Internet have already started with major banks linking with software houses to provide secure mechanisms for electronic payments, supermarkets offering travel-free shopping and bookstores breaking new ground in retailing an old technology through a new one. The glimmerings of the future are already here. Nevertheless many business people are sceptical about the possibilities of generating sales over the Internet.

Why is the current reality not quite what the pundits and consultants would have us believe?

First, the Internet can still be a baffling place for all but the informed and irritating for all the but the patient. It can take time to find the site you want and it is common to come across hyperlinks that don't work because the 'site is still under development', or because the server 'does not recognise that address'. When you do get to sites, they can take a long time to display if they contain a lot of graphical information.

Second, early experimentation, which included the setting up of cyber-shopping malls, showed that shoppers were reluctant to shop that way. This was because the goods weren't as varied as in the real shops; shoppers could not try the goods out by seeing, touching, or tasting; or they needed the social mix of actually 'being there'. One early experiment by Barclays Bank – BarclaySquare – is said to have netted no more than a corner-shop would have done.

Third, although consumers are happy enough to give their credit card numbers over the phone, they have been hesitant to do so over the Web. The problem is one of knowing that the seller really is who they say they are, and that your credit card number is not disappearing into a black hole, or into the clutches of a fraudster. Various authorities are warning online shoppers of the risk of bogus Web sites, designed to look real ones, but which are easily set up with the sole purpose of obtaining your credit card details. The problem is similar for the seller who wants to be assured that the buyer is authentic and the credit card really does belong to them. Buying and selling on the Web depend on authentication and verification as well as on security and confidentiality.

Fourth, the pundits' talk of 'global' markets is misleading. Only 7% of the world's population have a telephone line and only a percentage of those 7% are connected to the Internet. It makes better marketing sense to tailor selling efforts to specific, identifiable markets rather than the general, a concept that is only just being embraced on the Internet.

Fifth, not all items are suitable for selling on the Internet. It is far easier to sell information products and services than hard goods. This is due – in part – to the nature of distribution. In this current phase of Internet development, the Web is benefiting those industries which are information-rich – like books, music and software, which don't rely on the sense of touch and feel, and which are closest to mail-order. Supermarkets are experimenting with home shopping, but some consumers who buy in this way, find that they have to pay a premium to have the goods delivered. So far, buyers seem happier to accept on-line ordering in the traditional mail-order sectors.

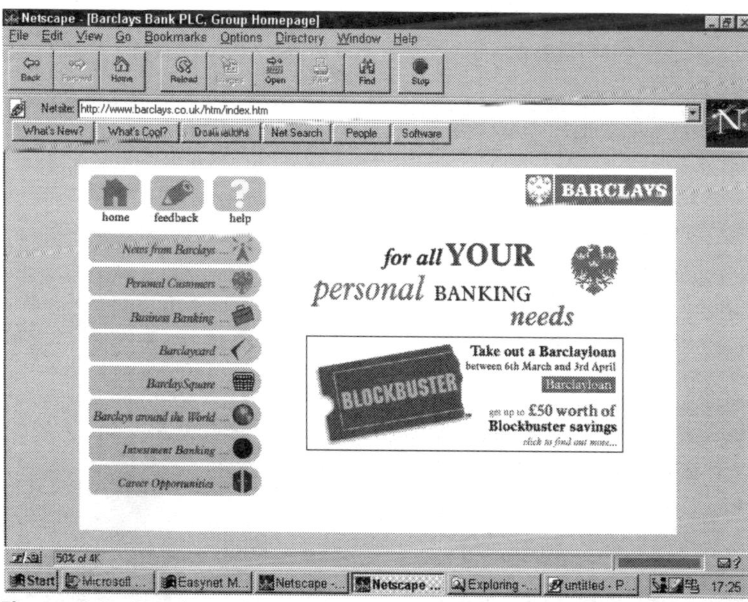

Figure 9.1 Barclays Bank with a direct link to the BarclaySquare Shopping Mall.

9.4 Future trends

There are several reasons why the current picture should change in line with the forecasts for the next millennium, referred to above.

More and more people are using the Internet and are becoming more knowledgeable about it. Also, telecommunications are improving and costs are falling, increasing access speeds, and Web site producers are becoming more serious about the overall quality of their sites.

Consumers lead increasingly busy lives and may become more amenable to online shopping as the range of goods on offer improves. As more people begin to shop this way, methods of distribution will change and costs of home delivery will fall.

Banks world-wide have put major investments into electronic payment systems. Most major banks in the UK, Europe and the USA, including VISA and MasterCard are working with software houses to finalise secure payment systems. Most companies in the Fortune 500 are now exploring the potential of a Web site for electronic marketing and trading. The infrastructure for such trading is still expensive but prices will fall as more companies take it up and the banks recoup their investment.

Marketers are waking up to the idea that marketing must be tailored to specific groups as in other media. Consumers too will get better at knowing which sites they want to visit and what they will find when they get there. Web sites are beginning to add value beyond what consumers can find in the terrestrial shopping world.

In terms of business-to-business marketing, the Internet can save time and money over traditional means by offering a buying medium which is unconstrained by the barriers of time or place. If you can specify your own requirements for product modification, agree them, negotiate over price and delivery all from your own back-yard, 24 hours a day, seven days a week, it is much quicker and cheaper for you and for the manufacturer.

9.5 What's selling?

Surveys show that some industries are learning – or are more suited to adapt – to take advantage of the Internet.

Financial services is a growing Internet sector where consumers can get advice from a wide range of service providers at lower prices than in the terrestrial world.

Well-established *banks and building societies* are at the forefront of new developments:

- Eagle Star is offering motor insurance online with discounts of up to 15% on traditional rates.
- Nationwide and the Royal Bank of Scotland are both offering full Internet banking services. In the case of fraud the RBS has said that it will foot the bill.
- Barclays Bank is another early Internet market-leader.
- Halifax offers travel insurance through its Web site by allowing people to tailor the policy to their needs. Enter a credit card number and the deed is done.

Many others are following their path.

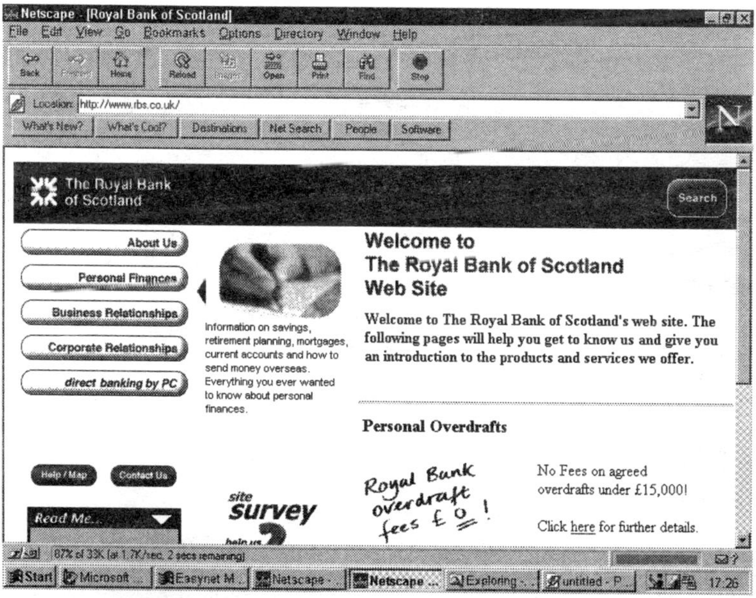

Figure 9.2 The Royal Bank of Scotland Home Page introducing direct home banking via your PC.

The *travel industry* has also adapted well to online communications. The travel agent's ability to use the networks to find the most suitable routes at the most competitive prices outplays the individual's advantage in dealing directly with the supplier.

Erotica and pornography have also grown on the Web. Whilst governments seek controls and software is developed to block unsuitable material, the industry has found its niche on the Web because it offers a privacy and an anonymity which the real world does not. Sad though it may be, the sex industry can teach its more respectable counterparts a Web lesson: discover the drawbacks of service in the real world and get the Web to counter them.

The *advertising* sector is beginning to get to grips with the potential of the Internet, as we saw in the last chapter (Section 8.3.12) with banner, button and keyword advertising. Advertising revenues are at the centre of many of the forecasts and projections.

The *retail* sector is learning to exploit the Web to reach new markets.

Figure 9.3 Tesco Supermarket offering a wider scope of services than would appear from a real visit.

Large stores such as Tesco and Sainsbury are both piloting online shopping with shoppers able to select from 20,000 items and have the goods delivered within the locality for a small fee.

But small shops too are using imagination and inventiveness to operate on the Web. A bakery in Whitby, North Yorkshire, monitors weather forecasts to quick-think what customers will want, rain or shine.

An example of an enterprising site, which trics to re-create and add value to the sale which would take place in the real world, is called **Bras Direct** (http://www.brasdirect.co.uk) which enables the visitor to select one of the bras in the collection and have it presented on an on-screen model.

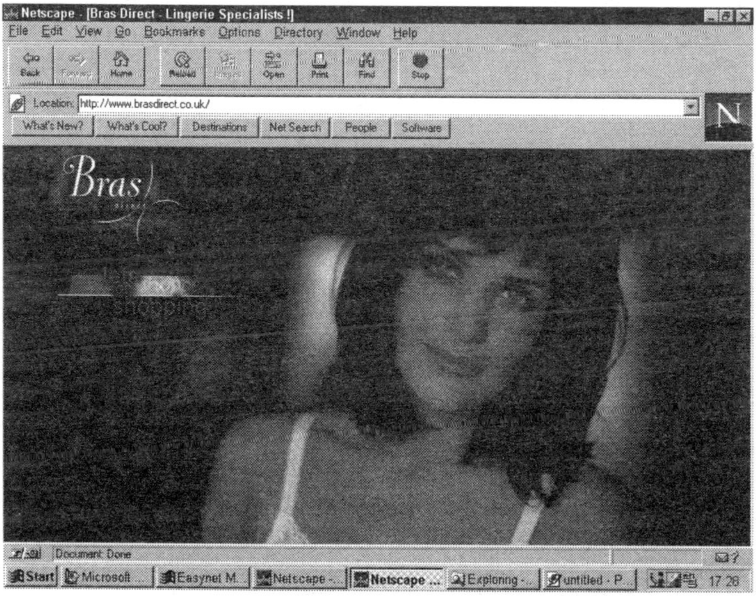

Figure 9.4 Bras Direct: selection, followed by mail order.

The visitor can zoom in to examine the bra in greater detail or change the colour of the one being displayed. This site takes credit card orders, like Amazon (see below), and delivers within three days of order.

Other diverse enterprising money-making initiatives include flower deliveries, pizzas to order, military models, and funeral arrangements.

Bookselling: **Amazon Books** (http://www.amazon.com) claims to be the largest bookshop in the world with over 2 million titles, but it really only keeps a couple of hundred of the most popular titles in stock. We saw a first glimpse of Amazon in Chapter 6. Figure 9.5 shows another screen further into the site.

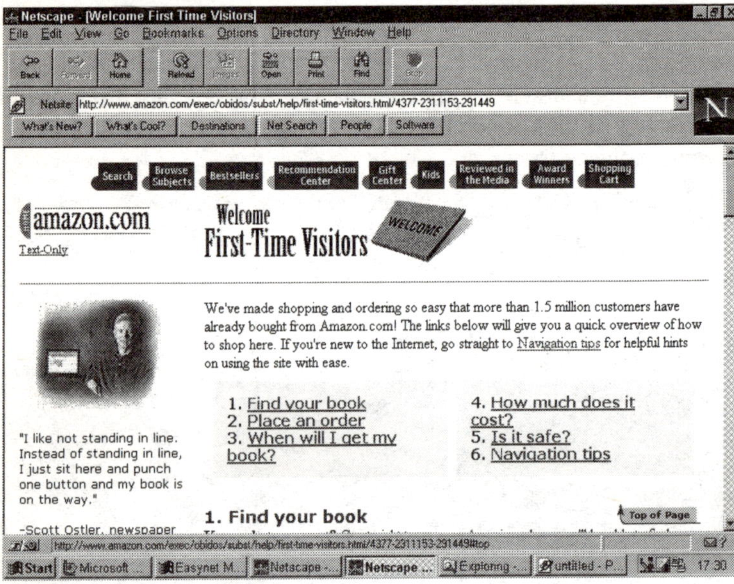

Figure 9.5 Internet shops are addressing customer concerns for security.

Amazon orders most titles from a nearby distributor and the rest direct from publishers, enabling Amazon to pass on substantial discounts on the list price. Amazon, however, is about more than just buying books; it offers reviews from the media and asks visitors to add their own. The site also includes extracts from books and has links to other books by the same author or on similar subjects. It offers other sites a percentage of each sale they direct to the site in their 'Associates program'. Amazon has built up an accurate database of customer preferences and buying patterns linked to their e-mail and postal addresses.

9.6 Paying electronically

Progress towards full electronic commerce has been hampered by hackers who have broken systems promising confidentiality and security. Although these cases have been few and far between and have required endless patience and enormous resources in their bid to be successful, they have nonetheless been rewarded by widespread publicity – often out of scale with the nature of their achievement.

There are a number of initiatives tackling these security concerns – EDI or electronic data interchange; e-cash or cybercash; and encryption systems. Between them, they promise to change the face of how buying and selling take place; we shall look at each of them in turn.

EDI

At its simplest, electronic data interchange is a form of electronic business-to-business purchasing which enables business to carry out ordering and selling safely. It requires a private network connection between two trading partners with an established trading relationship. In the past this has usually limited EDI to larger companies able to afford the network connection: many of the Fortune 500 companies use EDI in one form or another.

This established form of electronic trading is adapting to the Web thanks to General Electric's experiment with their Trading Process Network (TPN). TPN software enables buyers to specify which suppliers should receive requests for bids, what should be included in the bid, managing the bids when they come back and notifying the successful suppliers. By taking EDI onto the Web, TPN opens up the trading process to a far wider variety of bidders and tenders because even small businesses without expensive network lines can compete through a standard Internet link-up.

E-cash

Many potential consumer transactions, meanwhile, involve small and anonymous purchases. These would be purchases for which you would not normally use a credit card, such as a newspaper or a magazine. It is claimed, therefore, that electronic markets need their own currency – digital money that is as safe and secure as the real thing and used like cash for small purchases. People would be more willing to pay over the Web for the odd item – so the argument went – if the sum involved were minor.

Experiments with cybercash – or e-cash – started in the mid-1990s with firms like First Virtual, DigiCash, and CyberCash pushing out similar but competing schemes. An e-cash account works quite simply:

Customers open an account with an e-bank i.e. one of the firms above, store their e-cash on their hard disk or in the bank's computer and use a pass code to authorise payment of goods.

It may be that e-cash is still ahead of the game. There are comparatively few takers as yet and most of those are individuals and shops who were involved in the controlled trials. The firms that kick-started the idea went public but their value has dropped to a fraction of the original worth. So why has it – so far – failed?

One suggestion is that people expect low-cost information to be free – especially on the Web – and they do not like to pay-as-you-go, even for small amounts. It is too open-ended for many budgets. People tend to prefer a flat subscription-type fee because it is limited and they know the full cost in advance.

Another possibility is the failure to publicise such schemes and consumers' continuing reluctance to shop online.

Credit card payments and encryption

The first experiments to secure credit card payments channelled the card numbers direct to a computer protected by a firewall so that they are simply not accessible to any other parties cruising the Internet. Firewalls are generally considered safe.

Encryption is perhaps the most promising way of making credit card payments secure - it is certainly the one which has attracted the most publicity, and investment. Encryption is the term used for scrambling messages so that only the intended recipient can decode and read them.

Banks have collaborated with major software firms to make encryption work.

A common form of encryption – SSL – has been used by banks and retailers to transmit financial data. Those using SSL say that it would take years to crack an encrypted message and that SSL offers as much, if not more, security than a telephone mail-order transaction.

Encryption techniques have made significant progress since the earlier experiments. Visa and MasterCard have collaborated on an encryption technology – Secure Electronic Transmission (SET) – that promises to make credit card payments safer than they are in the real world. SET offers virtually uncrackable encryption and requires both sender and recipient to have software supplied by the card issuer to prove to each other that they are who they claim to be. SET verifies that the retailer is qualified to take credit cards and shields the card numbers from the retailer, keeping them encrypted all the way to the bank. This not only provides security but also the authentication that buyer and seller require of each other.

SET provides an Internet industry standard for online trading and offers organisations a Kitemark symbol indicating that online buying and selling are safe.

Although it is estimated that some 80% of European banks will offer a full Internet banking service by the year 2000, electronic trading still needs the boost of trust and confidence to carry it beyond experimentation into widespread practice.

In late 1997, an official-looking advertisement, seemingly from Yahoo – one of the leading search engines – promised free modems to randomly selected users who were requested to reply with their credit card numbers to pay for postage and packing. It turned out to be a fake and the real Yahoo reacted quickly to shut down the bogus account.

Many pushing – and using – encryption in order to carry out financial transactions say that the adverse publicity has grown out of all proportion and that it is only normal to knock that which is new, especially if it is electronic. Jim Barksdale, the boss of Netscape, is quoted as saying that he knows of no-one who has lost any money on the Internet.

Golden Keys

Depending on which browser you are using, an icon – representing a golden key or golden padlock – should appear in the bottom left of the screen. When this symbol is solid – not broken – it indicates that the credit card information will be encrypted, appearing only as a random set of numbers or characters and thus secure from use by any third party. Only the authorised merchant, or bank, will have the key to unlock the figures at the other end.

Icons such as these, representing secure transactions between traders who have identified each other, are key symbols to build confidence in electronic trading.

We have seen many examples of this, mainly with the key broken.

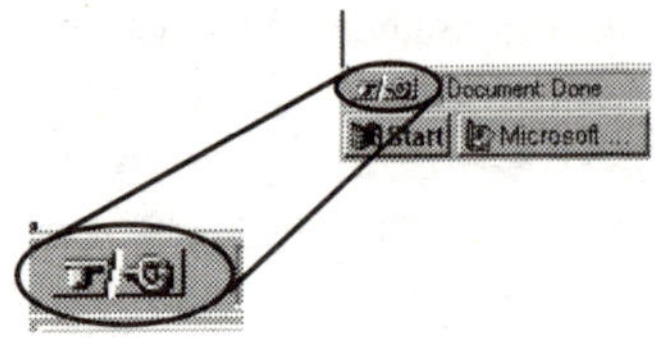

Figure 9.6 The Golden Key icon in Netscape when visiting a site that does not support encryption.

Stories of successful hackers are diminishing and with major banks and insurance companies now plunging into the electronic deep-end, we are beginning to see a climate of growing confidence. This is being built not only through the weight of investment of financial institutions in the electronic future, but also by the fact that some, such as the Royal Bank of Scotland, are willing to accept liability in the event of a fraud.

9.7 Buying and selling on the Web

With a growing number of organisations demonstrating different ways and means of making money on the Web, and with banks on the point of assuring safe and secure payment transactions, how do we go about selling, and buying, on the Web?

1 Find out your customer preferences for payment along with their buying habits and patterns. If they are gearing up for trading on the Web, then your message is clear. If they are not, then it is equally clear, but useful to find out why not. What are the obstacles holding them back?

2 Determine whether or not your products or services are suitable for electronic transactions and mail-order? How much are they information-rich? On the other hand, how much do they need some kind of inspection before buying, like trying on a pair of shoes, or inspecting the quality of foodstuffs?

Even if they are not ideally suited on the surface, for example selling tractors or JCBs to the farming community, this does not mean that a Web site is out of the question. Many firms have won business from unexpected quarters because their site offers a shop-window to customers who would normally not come across their products. Remember that the shop-window can be an effective support to purchasing decisions.

3 Find out whether you can afford the infrastructure necessary for electronic trading. This is particularly important where individual sales are of low value. Keep an eye on these costs as they are likely to drop.

4 If you decide to go down the trading route think about the tactics you will need to create a shopping community. Think about how you can reassure your customers that they are safe in your hands and that their credit-card payment is secure. If it is not, then perhaps you should think twice, or provide them with a warning that it is better to pay via traditional methods.

5 Talk to your bank about their plans for electronic trading and how they can help you. Without their support and advice, it is probably better to stick to a shop-window, whether selling or buying.

9.8 Summary

The Web is on the verge of building a potential trading community of millions of buyers and sellers. With many organisations beginning to take advantage of the security that encrypted systems can bring, it is now a case of building consumer confidence on a wider scale. This will be affected in part by the extent to which regulations protecting the consumer are applied on the Internet. We look at the law and the Internet in the next chapter.

10 THE INTERNET AND THE LAW

10.1 Aims of this chapter

The laws and codes of practice which lay down what you can and cannot do, should and should not do, in the real world, pertain just as much to the Internet. They apply to misleading advertising, to sellers' obligations, to buyers' rights and to the ownership of information.

Although regulations are difficult to interpret and enforce – and many are being continually debated and revised by the US Senate as well as by the European Commission – they apply nonetheless. In this chapter, we shall look at various aspects of legal regulation of business on the Internet.

10.2 Advertising and selling

As the Web becomes an increasingly effective and competitive market-place, consumer rights and seller obligations are correspondingly growing areas of interest. It is important to remember that although the Internet exists only in computer- or cyber-space, the laws of the real world still apply. Any organisation putting information on the Web for marketing and advertising purposes has a duty to respect standard advertising practice, and ensure that the content of their information is accurate and up-to-date.

In the UK, the Sales Promotion Code and the Advertising Standards Authority's Advertising Code apply equally to the Web as they do to traditional media. They are not legally binding but most organisations which breach such codes are willing to toe the line when challenged. This is because it is mostly in their interest to make the Web a place where consumers can shop in confidence. Further sanctions exist in the form of legislation – in the UK – with the Control of Misleading Advertisements Regulations1988, which enables the Office of Fair Trading to take action against anyone publishing a misleading advertisement.

As a general rule, Web advertisements are subject to the laws and regulations of the country where the site is accessed; this can lead to liability under local law. Virgin Atlantic Airways was fined under United States advertising regulations for offering out-of-date price information on its Web site.

If you are intending to tackle world-wide markets, then it makes sense to have your site available in the languages of the markets you are targeting. If, however, such a foreign-language advertisement were found to be misleading under the local law of that country, the seller might have difficulty claiming honourable intentions. In 1996, a US court held one Italian company to be infringing a US trademark, simply by offering access to its Web site to Americans.

On the Web, due care and research over the proprietary nature of trade marks and names should also be extended to domain names. Some organisations have found another using their registered trade name as a domain name or address on the Web. This has even extended as far as the Internet regulators themselves. Recently US Federal regulators accused one Australian firm of deception for selling Internet domain names. The domain name adopted by the Australian firm is curiously similar to the official US body in charge of registering and maintaining Internet Domain names. The US authorities are requiring the Australian firm to stop using the Internic address and refund fees to some 2,000 customers. This may have been done from sheer ignorance or innocence; on the other hand, it may have been a deliberate ploy to attract custom by deception.

10.3 Consumer protection

Provided that the company which sold you goods is located in the UK, British law makes no distinction about how you bought it – you are given the same level of protection whether it was by phone, face-to-face in a shop or via the Web.

In the European Union, people are also protected under the Brussels convention in dealings with companies based in other countries of the EU. Although the onus of proof is on the customer, a European Union citizen can take action in any EU country against a company situated in any other member state. Currently, anyone buying from within the EU from a country outside it has no real consumer protection.

The European Distance Selling Directive, adopted by the European Commission in February, 1997 is likely to come into effect before the year 2000. It will require all Web vendors to ensure that their terms and conditions for trading are easily accessible, even obligatorily displayed, on screen. Crucially, these terms and conditions will have to state under which country's legal jurisdiction the sale is made. The Directive will require sellers to provide information including:

- their name and address;
- detailed information about the product;
- arrangements for delivery and payment;
- time of delivery and what happens if delivery is late;
- who bears the risk if the product is lost or damaged.

For some products – excluding information-rich products such as software or electronic magazines – the customer will have the right to withdraw from any sales contract within one week.

If there is a risk of difficulty in meeting stated delivery terms, it may be advisable to make it clear on the Web site that the company is not making an offer to supply goods, but rather an invitation to the customer to make an offer to purchase.

10.4 Taxation

We have seen projections for electronic trading turnover amounting to hundreds of billions of $US, and electronic commerce of all shapes and kinds is indeed increasing on a daily basis. So what about tax?

The US Treasury and the UK Inland Revenue both estimate revenue losses in billions due to the growth of computer trading. At present it is unknown exactly how much is not being collected simply because there are no accurate trading figures – no one knows how to collect them or how to collect the tax. Tax, however, is due; but the problem is relatively complex.

Tax laws are based on geography – where the company is located, or doing business, and on the products and services being sold. The Internet is changing one's conception of geography – where is cyberspace? – and one's notion of a product or service – no longer something you can always touch and feel.

Tax laws are also based on a distinction between goods and services. If the

Internet is used for ordering and paying for goods and services – to take a UK example – usual VAT rules should apply. But if the Internet is also the medium for delivering the product, such as downloading a film, music or a book, then VAT is not so simple to apply. A book in print, for example, is zero-rated for VAT in the UK, but if you were to download it from the Internet, it attracts VAT at the full rate because it is deemed to be the supply of a service. The problem intensifies with cross-border trade and differing applications of purchase or value added tax. The levying of customs duties also hinges on whether material which can pass through the Internet, is classified as a good or a service. At present, however, both EU and US officials believe that the Internet should be a customs free zone. If the World Trade Organisation agrees, all levies on electronic transmissions will be legislated against.

While tax authorities grapple with the anomalies of electronic commerce, other initiatives explore a 'bit tax' under which each electronic transmission – fax, phone call, e-mail – could be logged and taxed. A bit tax, applying to each digital unit sent over the Internet, irrespective of its content, would mean a shift away from value-added tax to one based purely on the quantity of data transmitted. This may seem 'unfair' on the one hand; on the other, if trading rules are changing, it is likely that tax rules will follow suit.

10. 5 Copyright

The law of copyright – flouted or ignored for decades – is gaining a new significance with electronic information transfer possible at the click of a button.

Technological developments have now far outstripped the capacity of copyright legislation to control the reproduction and transmission of intellectual property. This issue continues to stretch the legislative bodies of the EU and of the US Senate as the focus of copyright shifts from not merely copying a document to encompass also that of transmitting it.

As soon as any intellectual property – be it text, images, graphs, video or music – is available through the Internet, then any monetary value attached to it is at risk. This is beginning to change with the payment mechanisms explained in the last chapter, although the hitherto 'free' ethos of the Internet has already led to an increase in what is available without charge as well as significant discounting in pricing policies.

While you would wish to attract site visitors by making certain information available to all-comers, be wary too, of making your valuable documentation free over the Web; it could rapidly lose – for you – any commercial value you attach to it.

When a customer pays for and receives a document on the Internet, it is only copyright law that stands in the way of instant modification, reproduction or selling on. An electronic document can be re-transmitted to hundreds or thousands of others on e-mail, newsgroups or via a Web site. Copyright transgressions are hard enough to monitor and control in the real world; on the Internet, it is virtually impossible to enforce copyright law without relying on 'good citizenship' to help the aggrieved party.

Although we tend to think here about material published in books and magazines, don't limit yourself to too narrow a view of 'publishing'. Anyone who sends an e-mail or puts information on a web site can be considered to be publishing, so, if it's not your information, you should not be using it without permission. Oasis, the pop group, issued a warning in May 1997 to all unofficial Oasis Web sites that legal action would result if unauthorised use of copyright material continued.

Be wary too about what you say about whom because there is also risk of defamation. Norwich Union Insurance was fined £450,000 for defaming a competitor, not on the Norwich Union Web site, but by passing untrue rumours about a competitor on its internal e-mail system!

Copyright can be horrendously complex, but there are basically two things to remember:

1 Documents that you, or your organisation have produced, are yours to dispose of in any appropriate legal manner.
2 Documents produced by others are not available for you to use, modify, copy, or re-transmit without permission or a licence from, or payment to, the producer, author or publisher.

Some have said that the Internet will bring about a massive change to copyright legislation, others that the force of copyright itself will influence the nature of business on the Internet. It is not yet certain what the outcome will be.

10.6 Privacy of the individual

While copyright protects others' intellectual property, the Data Protection Act came into force in the UK in 1984 to provide rights to people about whom personal information is held on others' computers (although the Act is being amended to include personal information held in all forms, not just that held on computer). The Act requires those who record and use data about individuals to be open about that use and follow practice laid down by the Data Protection Registrar.

One of the great advantages of the Web is that site owners can track what customers look at, buy or reject, and can obtain information such as name, address, or preference, etc. This is possible because when you visit an Internet site, you leave your own domain name as a calling-card. This is known as IP address logging, and some view it as an invasion of privacy. It is, however, fundamental to the way the Internet works – a visitor's address has to be known by the host site, otherwise it would not know where to direct any information requested. Information can also be collected in other ways, including visitor registration forms, and, more controversially, cookies.

COOKIES

A cookie is a piece of information that a Web site can send out which can be unknowingly stored on your hard-drive. It can store information on your preferences at that site, which can be collected by the Web site sender at a later date. Used principally to pick up marketing information about your preferences, cookies are a violation of an individual's privacy, even if used for generally 'ethical' purposes.

A cookie sits on your hard drive under the filename *cookies.txt* and can be deleted. Browsers can be configured to alert you to the arrival of a cookie, or to disable them, and there are programs, e.g .Cookie Crusher and Cookie Crumbler, which will reject all cookies.

Some Web site owners are starting to announce that theirs is a 'cookie-free' site.

Such information can be construed to be personal information, use of which – in the UK – is subject to data protection legislation. The Data Protection Registrar requires to know about the:

- Personal data held by the data user
- Sources of that personal data
- Purposes for which the personal data may be used
- People to whom the data may be disclosed
- Overseas countries to which data may be transferred.

The Data Protection Registrar can insist that the data be collected fairly and lawfully, that it should not be excessive for the purposes stated, that it be accurate, up-to-date and not held longer than necessary, and that it be kept secure from intrusion.

10.7 A Framework for Global Electronic Commerce

In July 1997 in a proposal called 'A Framework for Global Electronic Commerce' (**http://www.ecommerce.gov/framewrk.htm**), President Clinton outlined the basic rules for international electronic commerce, including making the Internet a duty-free, untaxed zone for electronic buying and selling. The framework – tantamount to a written constitution for the Internet – consists of five principles and nine issues.

Principles

- The private sector should lead.
- Governments should avoid undue restrictions on electronic commerce.
- Where governmental involvement is needed, its aim should be to support and enforce a predictable, minimalist, consistent and simple legal environment for commerce.
- Governments should recognise the unique qualities of the Internet.
- Electronic commerce over the Internet should be facilitated on a global basis.

Issues

Customs and taxation

Taxation of Internet sales should neither distort nor hinder commerce. Any tax system should neither discriminate among types of commerce nor create incentives to change the nature or location of transactions.

Electronic payment systems

Inflexible and highly pre-scriptive regulations and rules are inappropriate and potentially harmful. Where marketplace and industry self-regulation do not fully address all the issues, government should ensure the safety and soundness of electronic payment systems, to protect consumers, or to respond to important law enforcement objectives.

'Uniform Commercial Code' for electronic commerce

Parties should be able to do business with each other on the Internet under whatever terms and conditions they agree upon. In order to enable participants in the marketplace to define and articulate most of the rules to govern electronic commerce, governments should encourage the development of simple and predictable domestic and international rules and norms that will serve as the legal foundation for commercial activities in cyberspace.

Intellectual property protection

In order to promote electronic commerce, sellers must know that their intellectual property will not be stolen and buyers must know that they are obtaining authentic products. The Administration understands the sensitivities associated with copyright management information and technological protection measures, and is working to tailor implementing legislation accordingly. Copyright-related objectives will include ensuring that US trading partners establish laws and regulations that provide adequate and effective protection for copyrighted works, including motion pictures, computer software, and sound recordings, disseminated via the Global Information Infrastructure (GII), and that these laws and regulations are fully implemented and actively enforced.

Privacy

The GII, if not managed carefully, can diminish personal privacy through its ease of re-using and re-transmitting information. It is essential, therefore, to assure personal privacy if people are to feel comfortable doing business. Principles of privacy, building on the OECD Guidelines Governing the Protection of Privacy and Transborder Data Flow of Personal Data, should ensure that data-gatherers inform consumers what information they are collecting, and for which purpose, and offer consumers meaningful ways to limit use and re-use of personal information.

Security

The GII must be secure and reliable. If Internet users do not have confidence that their communications are safe from unauthorised access or modification, they will be unlikely to use the Internet on a routine basis for commerce. There is no single 'magic' technology that ensures that the GII will be secure and reliable. Accomplishing that goal requires a range of technologies (encryption, authentication, password controls, firewalls, etc.) all supported by trustworthy management infrastructures.

Telecommunications infrastructure and information technology

Global electronic commerce depends upon a modern, seamless, global telecommunications network. Governments need to encourage private sector investment by

- privatising government-controlled telecommunications companies
- promoting competition to monopoly phone markets, ensuring interconnection at fair prices
- guaranteeing open access to networks on a non-discriminatory basis
- implementing pro-competitive and flexible regulation that keeps pace with technological development.

Content

While supporting the broadest possible free flow of information across international borders, the framework recognises that the GII medium offers greater opportunities for users to shield themselves from offensive or inappropriate material in comparison to traditional broadcast media. The Administration therefore supports industry self-regulation, adoption of competing rating systems, and development of easy-to-use technical solutions (e.g. filtering technologies and age verification systems) to assist in screening information online.

Advertising

The rules of 'country-of-origin' should serve as the basis for controlling Internet advertising to alleviate national legislative roadblocks and trade barriers.

Fraud

The Administration will explore opportunities for international cooperation to protect consumers and to prosecute false, deceptive, and fraudulent commercial practices in cyberspace.

Technical standards

Standards are critical to the long-term commercial success of the Internet as they can allow products and services from different vendors to work together. The United States believes that the marketplace, not governments, should determine technical standards and other mechanisms for interoperability. Technology is moving rapidly and governments' attempt to legislate or regulate can inhibit technological innovation. There need not be one standard for every product or service associated with GII, and technical standards need not be mandated. In some cases, multiple standards will compete for marketplace acceptance. In other cases, different standards will be used in different circumstances.

The success of electronic commerce will require an effective partnership between the private and public sectors, with the private sector in the lead.

There is a great opportunity for commercial activity on the Internet. If the private sector and government act appropriately, this opportunity can be realised for all people.

(Adapted from *A Framework for Global Electronic Commerce*, The White House, July 1, 1997, http://www.ecommerce.gov.framewrk.htm).

10.8 Summary

Being aware of regulations, codes of good practice and government policy are as essential to your Internet strategy as knowledge of your business and of the Internet itself. Most companies – depending on their size – will not want to build a legal department, but one safety measure would be to invest in legal advice. Few managers can afford to ignore the legal framework in which the Internet operates.

11 INTRANETS AND EXTRANETS

11.1 Aims of this chapter

In this chapter we shall look at Intranets and Extranets to see how they can be put to use to build competitive advantage based on sharing and exploiting information and knowledge.

11.2 What are Intranets and Extranets?

Just as you can view text and graphics on the World Wide Web, download software or send and receive e-mail, so you can do the same within an organisation on an internal network, using the same tools and techniques. Such an internal system is known as an Intranet. Access is controlled by the organisation which owns it and is restricted to the employees of that organisation.

An Intranet is a private, corporate network based on the same technology as that of the Internet. It can act as a feed for the organisation's Web site but is also an important way of sharing knowledge between employees and with suppliers and other partners.

Information is held on a server and any computer attached to it can access all or some of the information. These computers may all be on the same geographical site or may be spread across regional, national or international boundaries. Usually they will all be owned by the same organisation.

There may, however, be some categories of people outside the organisation, for example suppliers, key customers, partners or groups of associated stakeholders who may be given access to certain parts of the Intranet designed specifically for them. This part of the system is referred to as an Extranet.

11.3 Why establish an Intranet?

The Intranet can serve four purposes:

To update the Web site

Collecting, preparing and updating information for a Web site is a substantial task for a Webmaster, particularly in a large organisation. An Intranet makes this easier because data can be transferred from the internal system to the external one. Of course, the success of the Intranet, and therefore its usefulness as a tool for updating the external Web site, will depend on everyone getting involved in it (see Section 11.6).

To exploit organisational information and knowledge

Intranets have become technically feasible at a time when organisations are starting to look at the best ways of exploiting the knowledge which they hold to improve their competitive advantage. This entails making not only their explicit knowledge (what is written down in documents such as company handbooks or patents) available in an easier and more accessible form but – what is more of a challenge – trying to capture some of their implicit knowledge (what is inside people's heads).

Intranets have the capability of improving knowledge transfer within an organisation in terms of wider accessibility, greater currency and speed.

To make partnership, customer or supplier relationships more effective

Internet technology in the form of an Extranet makes it possible for companies to communicate with their suppliers and agents more cheaply, more easily and more effectively. It also allows the participants to improve their relationship.

To facilitate new ways of working

These include such as cross-functional team-building and teleworking, which cut across barriers of time and space

See Chapter 13 for details on how Internet technology can change the way we work.

THE INTRANET – A CASE FOR DISTRIBUTION

Large-scale distribution companies can use an Intranet to update their product range from suppliers and to deliver accompanying documentation to client organizations. Before the advent of Intranets, such organizations probably experienced nightmares with paperwork. Collating pages of up-to-date information on fast-changing products from a variety of suppliers would often mean that the product did not match its description. If some suppliers were located overseas, this mismatch was compounded on an even grander scale with postal inconsistencies.

Using an Intranet, or part of it as an Extranet, the organization can improve its information flow by building better relationships with suppliers. Some organizations are tackling this by providing bio-pics – photographs and brief descriptions of who's who – on the Intranet. This can help to bridge the divide that inevitably exists between people who have never met and only speak to each other on the phone. Working diaries can also be made available so that Intranet/Extranet users know who is available, and when.

The Intranet can further benefit the case for distribution by sending orders directly to suppliers. In this way, the Intranet can help in making the Distributor an effective one-stop clearing-house without increasing stockholdings or logistics overheads.

11.4 Possible Intranet content

There are many kinds of information you can present on an Intranet. You might start with low level information such as:

- telephone lists;
- employee handbooks;
- induction material;
- product and service guides;
- organisation wide memos;
- specification guidelines;

- policies and procedures;
- a suggestion box;
- employee diaries;
- frequently asked questions by customers;
- notices of thanks (and complaints);
- press releases and incidents of press reporting;
- new product information.

Much of this consists of information which is purely for internal purposes. Some, such as the product and service guides may be developed for loading up to the Web site. Other items such as specification guidelines may be made accessible to some outsiders, such as suppliers, on the Extranet; the suggestion box may be an open platform available to all.

Intranet information might graduate to include knowledge databases which might contain information such as new projects in progress, who is working on what with which customers, or Who Knows What – A Directory of Expertise in the organisation.

The extent to which this kind of information is kept secure, or made available, depends on the culture of the organisation you work for, and the degree of risk with which you feel comfortable. Low-level information will be available to everyone, but sensitive or confidential project information may be put on restricted access. How much information you make available to suppliers and external partners on the Extranet will depend on how central they are to the development process and how far you can trust them with confidential information.

11.5 Advantages of Intranets

- Elimination of duplication of information and of confusion over which is the latest version of a document.
- Wider ownership of information is encouraged and there is greater pressure to make it accurate.
- Better customer service because the organisation is less 'departmentalised' and more integrated.
- More efficient information transfer at lower cost.

- Improved team-working and collaboration on projects because the Intranet provides a common working and reporting base.
- Increased potential for innovation and development because the Intranet provides a source of contacts.
- Improved product/service design because the Extranet keeps you in touch with customer views.
- Faster response times from employees, suppliers and customers which can lead to increased speed to market.

> *"Intranets allow organisations to install a cost-effective internal communication and information system with both a low risk and a high return on investment. The rapid payback is due to an improved information flow which in turn creates higher productivity through a highly informed workforce. There are also massive savings made in the area of reprographics."*
>
> Paul Blackmore, Manager of the Consultancy firm One Stop Information Services (OSIS) in *Information World Review*, May 1997, p.21.

11.6 Managing the Intranet

The extent to which these potential advantages can be realised depends on how the Intranet is managed. There are a number of factors to bear in mind before jumping in at the deep end.

Where it is intended to make the Intranet the primary source of information in the organisation, it is vital to keep it up-to-date. However much it is accepted that information is for sharing, some people are inveterate hoarders of information and see it – perhaps consciously, perhaps unconsciously – as a source of personal power. Others are just bad communicators. There is therefore a need to assess and improve the information-sharing culture of the organisation by persuading managers of the importance to them of information exchange and by rewarding information sharing on the part of employees.

There may be a tendency to try an approach which is intended to be comprehensive and sophisticated from the outset. Such an ambition will almost certainly fail. Go instead for early winners and build up the Intranet as people get used to the idea, and it takes root. Focus on continuing improvement, change and development.

Consult with specialists on the technicalities of the network and on the design of the Intranet. Many of the issues are similar to those we encountered in Chapters 3 and 8. Look at the Intranet as a project – at least for the start-up phase and think carefully about the stages of:

- Specification and design
- Task allocation, resourcing and budgeting
- Planning the milestone achievements, checking on progress and reporting
- Implementation and integration.

Think carefully about the type and level of detail that you want to put on the component parts of the Intranet. Does this involve information that:

- is going to be published on the Extranet, or the Web, or restricted to employees on the Intranet?
- is relatively confidential in some cases, or can it be made available to everyone?
- you wish to disseminate one-way only, or is it two-way involving the use of e-mail reply forms or conferencing through discussion groups?

Consider who is going to have the final responsibility for signing-off information on the system and who is going to be responsible for making sure that old information is replaced, updated, archived or dumped.

Plan a period of thorough demonstration and training to show your people what the advantages of the Intranet are. Keep these sessions free of jargon and focused on what people do and the way they can benefit. This is the key stage in making sure – as much as possible – that the Intranet will be integrated and assimilated into working practice.

11.7 Summary

An Intranet is based on Internet technology but is restricted to staff, and in some cases, the suppliers, partners and/or customers of the organisation which owns it.

Its primary purpose is to facilitate information exchange within an organisation but it also serves as a feed for the organisation's Web site.

It has tremendous potential to make an organisation more efficient and to exploit its knowledge assets.

In order to achieve this potential, however, it is as important to focus on the people issues associated with information sharing as on the technical issues of setting up an Intranet.

Next we look at developing an Internet strategy.

12 DEVELOPING AN INTERNET STRATEGY

12.1 Aims of this chapter

In the remaining chapters, we shall try to establish a way forward by stealing a glimpse of the Internet in the future and by looking at how it can change the way we work.

Developing a strategy for the Internet means assessing the Internet's weaknesses and opportunities, working out what you want to achieve and how best to tackle it and appraising your own strengths and weaknesses.

Strategic management has more do with how you achieve a vision for the future, than sticking to the present or past. More than anything else, it is about how you manage change.

Formulating an Internet strategy means:

- Gaining a perspective of the Internet of the future
- Carrying out some analysis on the past and present of your organisation
- Thinking where you want to be in the future and how you want to build towards that from the present.

12.2 The Internet: its weaknesses

"*The Internet was designed to survive a nuclear war. But can it withstand the perils created by its own rapid growth?*" (*McKinsey Quarterly*, 1997, No 1, p. 127)

What we want to achieve will depend very much on the view we have formed of the Internet – on exactly what kind of prospects it holds for us.

At one peak evening quarter-hour in May 1997, the people who logged into AOL – America Online, one of the major Internet Access and Service

Providers – outnumbered those watching CNN and MTV. If the Internet begins to eat away at the popularity of TV, is it already becoming the popular success that many have forecast? Or is becoming the victim of its own success? The answer to both questions, paradoxically, is yes. Such experiences have led AOL and other Service Providers to experience a growing amount of down-time and breakdowns.

The size of the Internet is increasing – the number of new users is growing at the rate of 120% p.a., the number of Web hosts at 100% p.a. and spending on products and services is rising at 110% p.a.

For many people, however, the Internet is at worst a non-event, shrouded in mystery, and at best characterised by anarchy and chaos. They point to:

- unregulated anarchy which allows pornography to sit by side with respectable information;
- information clutter and overload dominated by trivia;
- slow response times with delays at popular access points;
- much publicised breakdowns because of growing network congestion;
- a rate of innovation which seems too rapid for most to keep up with;
- a lack of hard evidence that money can be made from the Internet;
- a preference for TV – cable or satellite – as a more digestible alternative to the inconsistencies and difficulties of the Web.

If we were to adopt this negative perspective, then we would do well to leave the Internet alone as a waste of time, or, at best, wait and see for a little longer.

12.3 The Internet: its opportunities

Such a scenario, however, ignores many of the influences and signs of progress that we have touched on in this book. Drivers like:

- The continual growth and use of the Internet in all parts of the world.
- Continuing technological developments offering solutions to business questions.

- The investment made by major banks and software houses to develop the commercial side of the Web.
- Early commercial successes that many organisations have enjoyed.
- The promotion, pump-priming and legislative efforts of national governments and two of the major trading powers – the EU and the US.
- The entrepreneurial and commercial spirit which will not accept today's way of doing things as valid for tomorrow.

The positive scenario assumes that the Internet will become a reliable platform for conducting business as:

- Consumer purchasing confidence spreads as a result of secure payment systems.
- Effective protection is given to copyright information.
- Standards emerge from consortia of telecomms and software firms.
- A mix of government subsidy, telecomms investment and consumer payment begins to pipe high bandwidth into the home and office.
- Private networks, which are more secure and robust, link up to the Internet for those customers willing to pay for premium services.
- Affordable market-based pricing for access and usage emerges.
- The Internet establishes its own identity – or identities – and becomes as integrated in social and business life as the Press and TV.

We would argue that the Internet is not going to go away or crumble around us and that the rate of technological innovation will continue to drive the Internet into new areas of activity.

12.4 Models for business

There are currently a number of business models in evidence for the Internet:

1. **The Communications Model** – using the Internet primarily to allow greater flexibility and efficiency through e-mail.

2 **The Advertising Model** – using the organisation's Web site as a shop window, and paying for advertising banners on other sites and search engines.

3 **The Subscription Model** – offering unlimited access to a service or product, for example, a newspaper, magazine or current awareness updating service in return for payment of an annual sum. This is generally held to be more successful than the Pay-As-You-Go alternative (look back to Section 9.6).

   This third alternative assumes that people will pay for information on the Web. As yet, they generally seem reluctant to do so.

4 **The Niche Marketing Model** – packaging personalised information, news and entertainment services. Here, as a superior alternative to TV, the Web provides an experience for selected groups of people – communities – through its interactive, two-way capability. In order to take full advantage of the multi-media, customers will need to have higher bandwidth – perhaps via ISDN – piped into the home.

   Niche services also include the gathering, tailoring and packaging of information to meet individuals' requirements, cutting out the trivia and pumping selected items through to the subscriber's e-mail box. This option will require the customer to put reservations about privacy aside and share personal preferences with the provider service.

5 **The Department Store Model** – setting up as a seller on the Web. This option sees the major obstacles to electronic commerce overcome and confidence in online buying and selling widespread. Customers can buy products direct from the producer, bringing prices down. New retailers will emerge bringing greater competition to the established market leaders with knock-on effects on pricing. The Financial Services sector has already witnessed this.

These scenarios paint alternative pictures of the future and there are no doubt others. Strategic planning means guesstimating as accurately as possible which of these options are most likely to become feasible, sooner or later.

12.5 Twelve strategic principles

1 Understand how the Internet works and what its potential is by experimenting with it, reading about it and discussing it with others.

2 Consider how the Internet can benefit your customers and keep your business moving forward. This means having a full understanding of your business and what it is trying to achieve. At first your aims may be fairly moderate – keeping up with the Joneses, or gaining more publicity – but begin to think more laterally about where the real advantages might lie in:

- access to wider markets
- cost savings and greater efficiencies in communication and distribution
- better customer information and service.

3 Start in a small way – getting started is more important than getting it perfect. List things you want to achieve in order of priority, having consulted your staff, suppliers and customers.

4 Obtain commitment from senior management – it is vital in all change and project management. So is everybody's involvement. You won't get anywhere by making the Internet a sideline that only a few know about and contribute to. Staff need time to feel their way and become familiar with the way the Internet works. Recognise that you will need expertise of a technical, design and legal nature.

5 Decide how much resource you can, or are prepared to, put into the Internet.

6 Expect your Website to be a cost-centre. Don't just look for sales. Value also those activities which lead indirectly to sales, such as generating enquiries from prospective clients.

7 Understand your audience – the profile of your best prospect is the profile of your best customer. Keep an eye on customer buying habits and the level of interactivity they are likely to want. Think about what customers most want to know about your organisation and what you most want to know about them. Think about why they use you instead of a competitor. The Web offers a new opportunity to build customer loyalty.

8 Think about how the Internet can add value to your services and products. This might lie in better information provision, alternative methods of distribution or more customisation for individuals and groups.

9 Align and integrate your Internet activities with all the others you perform in the real world for the benefit of customers and staff alike.

10 Think about control policies and procedures which make it clear:

- Who may access the Web and who may not, and why?
- What information may be imported from the Web into the organisation's systems?
- Who has ownership and responsibility for information on the Web?

Consider how the power-base in the organisation may change as staff increasingly have direct access to information which can change not only the way work is done, but also what work is done.

11 Monitor the effects of your Internet strategy. Look at the levels of e-mail and Web activity in the organisation, the cost-savings in staff-time, direct or indirect income, and customer reaction.

12 Keep your Internet services adaptable, changing and moving forward. This means taking risks, keeping up with new technological developments and exploring new possibilities.

12.6 Managing change

If one half of strategic management involves thinking through the changes needed, the other half is about making sure they work. The key to achieving this lies in how fit the organisation is for change.

The following offers a health-check of the key factors you have to get right if you are to cope with change – such as introducing the Internet to the organisation – on a substantial scale:

- **Values**: Is there a clear, long-term vision to which all stakeholders subscribe?

- **Leadership**: Does the leader set an example, act as a role model and foster learning and development?
- **Strategy**: Does everyone know what they are doing and why? How do they contribute to the overall goals of the organisation?
- **Customers**: Do we have good understanding of their needs and expectations?
- **Processes**: Which are the key systems and processes which give us our strength?
- **People**: Are our people developing, innovating and responsible?
- **Control**: Do measurement and procedural control stifle creativity?
- **Integration**: Do we have a business of people in separate boxes or do we mix across areas, functions and responsibilities?
- **Results**: Is our focus entirely on the short-term bottom-line or are we looking 5–10 years ahead, and investing for it?

Rules for managing change

There are no hard and fast rules for managing change, and there are certainly no magic formulas. But there is a body of accumulated practice and experience largely derived from where things have gone wrong in the past, or where people have taken the time to get it right.

Read at least one book which tackles change management, something by John Kotter or Rosabeth Moss Kanter, for example, even a quick how-to book. Reading a book will take a day or two – the change itself will take longer and cost a lot more – especially if you get it wrong.

Make the effort to:

- Carry out an organisational audit which involves present and future assumptions about key functions and systems, customer expectations and core skills and competencies.
- Think the change through. Be clear on what kind of change may affect people from a broader perspective: job content, responsibility, new/unknown tasks, new methods of working, new skills, new relationships, and new threats to job security.

- Set up a team of stakeholders, not top management, but the key people involved in designing and delivering the service as well as those receiving it.
- Create a sense of purpose and urgency to tackle problems which have prevented progress in the past. Ask what and who is preventing progress and who can really help in unblocking it? Think of breaking the code of silence that maintains the status quo. Loosen up control parameters to enable more creativity. Put conflict to work positively.
- Plan how to get top management committed, active, and consistent. Consider how to prepare employees for change by selling the advantages meaningfully, but acknowledging any downsides honestly. Plan how to win over resistance and convert the stagnant into the active, how to create effective ownership. Allow for things to go wrong.
- Go for specific objectives. Look for early wins – but not quick fixes. Identify who can help to achieve early success which demonstrates that change is working.

12.7 Summary

Strategy and change are highly interwoven – it is rare that one can work without the other. Before formulating a strategy for exploiting the Internet we need to consider its weakness as a business medium for the future, but also its opportunities. We can then think how we could best use the Internet to achieve our business goals. A framework for doing this has been outlined in this chapter. Next we look at how the Internet can change the way we work.

13 CHANGING THE WAY YOU WORK

13.1 Aims of this chapter

In this chapter we focus on how the Internet is changing – and has the potential to change – the way we work. This includes innovations in when and where work is done, bringing cost-savings, environmental benefits and greater flexibility to both employer and employee. These changes in turn raise issues of managerial control of, and trust in, employees.

We shall look at how the Internet can help organisations respond to changes in the marketplace and gain competitive advantage by facilitating:

- Greater innovation and creativity
- Flexible working
- Cross-functional team-working
- Alliances with other organisations.

13.2 The benefits of distance working

The Internet and other associated technologies, such as videoconferencing and computer-integrated telephony, have made a range of distance-working practices possible. We will look at these as this chapter progresses. It is important to recognise their significance in bringing a number of benefits to business:

Flexible working

The traditional way of working – 9 to 5, five days a week at the employer's premises – is no longer the most convenient for many employees and organisations. Various forms of remote working can be more suitable for staff who increasingly have to juggle work and home commitments and for employers looking for productivity improvements, cost-savings and better customer service.

Overcoming barriers of time and space

In the past, geographic factors created delays, costs or even impossibilities in the way business was conducted. These are no longer constraints in communicating with employees working away from base, with customers, and with other organisations, whether they be suppliers, partners or even rivals.

Cooperating with other departments and other organisations

Technology facilitates cross-functional and cross-organisational team-working. This means that managers can draw on talents from outside their own employee base as and when they are needed for specific projects.

Cost-savings

It has been estimated that savings of 25–30% can be made on office space using flexible working practices. Employees save on travel time and costs.

Environmental benefits

As fewer people travel to and from work everyday or move around for meetings, pollution damage from cars, trains and buses is reduced.

13.3 Teleworking

Teleworking is the term adopted to signify work carried out at a location remote from the workplace principally by using a computer and telecommunications equipment. This remote location may be the home, but not necessarily. Many organisations – attracted by the potential cost-savings in office-space and the flexibility it offers to the workforce – have explored the possibilities of teleworking and many more continue to try it out. People are more ready to work from home as the prestige of 'owning' office-space declines and as improvements to technology mean that remote workers are less isolated than in the past.

Although some companies employ people who work at home permanently, successful schemes show that a mix of teleworking and time spent at the office for briefing and social interaction can be a more practical combination. Such an arrangement also makes it easier for managers to monitor and motivate employees whom they no longer see face-to-face everyday.

Teleworking has enormous implications for management monitoring and control. When everyone used to come into the office, productivity and performance tended to be measured by time spent at the desk, manifested in clocking-in. But how do you ensure that work is being accomplished satisfactorily when you don't see people regularly, when you don't always know where they are, and when you can't be sure of what they are doing.

Some types of work are more suited to teleworking than others and some managers are still suspicious of the whole idea. Thankfully, however, we are moving away from 'peering over the shoulder' to check up on people, by exploring how we can best empower them with responsibility, for the benefit of the organisation.

Honesty and trust will have to play an even greater role if the benefits of teleworking are to become realised on a wider scale. More relevant appraisal measures than the quantity of work performed, relating instead to quality, initiative and innovation are becoming more important. Overall contribution to customer service and the strategic contribution of the individual are already developing in significance. When you are close to the customer, you are in the best position – whether you work at home, in the office or at a customer's premises – to make informed assessments about they want and what they might want next, because you have more complete information. The availability of information makes strategy everyone's business now.

Be wary of jumping in the deep end with teleworking; it's never too easy to backtrack. Plan a pilot first. Ensure that participants have some or many of the qualities and skills required for teleworking, such as self-discipline, trustworthiness, good time management and computer and telecommunications literacy. Check that people have the right equipment to do the job required at home and make sure that there are always the right facilities for teleworkers at work on 'office-days'. Think about the sense of belonging that all of us need and, above all, ensure that regular channels of communication are set up.

Telecentres

Teleworking is not necessarily confined to the home. The home might not be suitable for many reasons. It might also prove expensive to equip large numbers of homes with computing and telecommunications equipment.

In such situations, telecentres or telecottages can provide an answer. Such centres offer shared multimedia facilities and are either owned by one organisation to provide their employees with a local work environment or are independent and used by a range of employers.

Mobile Working

Mobile or nomadic workers, such as salespeople, consultants or service engineers, need the tools to access the same information as that available to desk-bound employees.

This requires an interchangeable use of mobile telephony, fax and e-mail for communicating, and remote access to the organisation's Intranet for efficient transfer and sharing of information. These tools enable the mobile worker to operate efficiently at home, in an office, on the road or in a hotel and win tangible benefits for the organisation. Salespeople can now process orders on the spot (providing they are empowered to negotiate and close deals) rather than having to return to the office and wait for a clerk to handle them.

Hot-desking

When the mobile or teleworker calls into the workplace they need a place to work which has all the facilities required.

With many conventional offices fully exploited for only a fraction of the time, some organisations have turned to hot-desking. Hot-desking means the removal of permanent, individual desks for some or all the employees. When staff turn up at the workplace, they are allocated a workstation from which they can access their networked computer messages and files.

With hot-desking, workspace is confined to drawers in filing cabinets or the use of a locker, and desks are booked and used as and when they are required. Facilities are made available for group activities or for people to meet, collect their mail and take part in socio-professional activities that play an important part in being at work.

Some organisations have introduced hot-desking not only to make cost-savings but also to introduce higher standards of service and equipment. A note of caution, however, some people resent the loss of their 'personal' space.

Hotelling

Hotelling extends the concept of hot-desking and comes into play when employees spend most of their time with customers rather than at the employer's premises. They may rely on their customers to provide a desk yet still stay in touch with colleagues at work by linking up on a laptop computer. When returning to work, they hot-desk.

13.4 The organisational power-base

We are moving rapidly into a period where employees are no longer rigidly grouped together, overseen and monitored as they were in the days of centrally administered systems. In today's working environment, the Internet and Intranets are enabling distributed information systems to put all the information necessary at the fingertips of those who need it to start and finish the job.

As more and more information is shared within and between organisations, it has become increasingly possible for employees to make their own judgements and challenge those of others. As a result the knowledge and power that go with information are no longer the privilege of the top.

This has a number of implications for the way people are managed as well as how they are organised.

Management style

The story of management style has been one of continuing evolution from an authoritarian and highly disciplined approach towards a consultative, participative and empowering approach that allows people to contribute to the decisions which shape what they do. New technologies, such as the Internet, along with other factors such as the delayering of organisations, has led to the participative approach emerging as the dominant one. Information puts the power-base of organisations with individuals and creates – like the Internet itself – an equal playing-field where strict adherence to the trappings of prestige and traditional authority no longer apply. The empowering style of the 1990s continues to be the foundation for many successful business initiatives.

13.5 The organisation of tomorrow

With continuing experiments into flexible working and empowerment, there are already a number of indicators that give a picture of how organisations are beginning to develop:

Co-operation

Because organisations can no longer move quickly enough or acquire all the resources to take on new product development projects with the speed that the market requires, there will be greater co-operation between organisations, some of which may even be, or have been, competitors.

Temporary alliances

In many cases, this co-operation will lead to the creation of temporary alliances where the organisation itself is not physically relocated, nor where people spend their time travelling to meet. Alliances can be seen as a pattern of linkages, connections or interactions between partnership organisations and individuals. Working from remote locations, people communicate by e-mail, voice mail, tele- or video-conferencing, or Web technology, as well as face-to-face.

Virtual teams

Sometimes, teams will come together composed of people who have never met and may never meet, who will be working on various other projects at the same time, who come from different levels and different functions as well as different locations and maybe different organisations. They will rely principally on using the Internet, or Internet technology, to keep in touch.

The individual and the organisation

Because individuals will be more mobile within and between organisations, the old hierarchical structures of the past will cede primacy to a flatter, more dispersed model. Organisations are becoming more flexible and fluid – described by some as organic – using cross-functional teams of people inside and outside the organisation, and dispersing them when the need for them is accomplished.

These teams and alliances – described as virtual organisations – rely on the free flow of information among the participants to stimulate learning and development. The success of the alliance depends largely on what knowledge is acquired from the others, assimilated and put to use. A new importance is therefore attached, not only to how information is conveyed but also to how it is received and acted upon, with acceptance and trust, or with scepticism.

13.6 Summary

Changing the way we work means recognising that the Internet can help to bring about a future which is discontinuous from the past.

We conclude with a snapshot of the future in Chapter 14.

14 PREPARING FOR THE FUTURE

14.1 Aims of the chapter

A bright technological future has been 'just around the corner' now for as long as we can remember. In the past, however, this promise disintegrated. But the Internet, through the convergence of technologies, has made the breakthrough. It is increasingly appealing to all sectors of the community – old as well as young, business people as well as entertainers, service providers as well as manufacturers, and unfortunately, the criminal as well as the law-abiding.

In this chapter we attempt to look at where the Internet will go next.

The first phase of Internet growth and development was dominated by the power of technology to change the way we do things. We shall look at current and imminent technologies that are continuing to transform the Internet. This first phase was also characterised by a lack of regulation and by criticisms of anarchy and chaos. We shall look at control options and raise some of the strategic issues which managers will have to address.

Just as the Internet has already made a significant impact on many of the ways that organisations do business, it has also made an impact on the skills people need in order that they may continue to make a contribution and remain employable. Finally, we shall look at management issues and those transferable skills deemed necessary for work in the 21st century.

14.2 Questions to be addressed

As the Internet continues to double in size, traffic congestion multiplies, delays in response times grow and breakdowns occur. Some have thought that with continual overloading of telecommunications networks, the Internet would collapse before the end of 1996.

Wrong maybe, but there are several lessons questions to ask:

Do pricing structures need to be changed?

With flat-fee pricing structures so widespread, users have no incentive to be economical. Whether you are online for five minutes or five hours, viewing text or moving pictures, you pay basically the same.

Does the Internet need more regulation?

There is no overall body in charge of the Internet; its laissez-faire spirit strives to hold onto its birthright as a 'free-for-all' society. Attempts by the US legislature to control 'questionable' material on the Web were rebuffed in 1997 by popular dissent.

Are higher bandwidth and better data-switching urgently needed?

There has been a continual shift towards more sophisticated applications – using colour, graphics, video and sound – which have led to performance degradation.

14.3 Market pricing

One increasingly likely option is for market-based pricing to segregate services and the networks that provide them, into those which users are willing to pay for and those which they are not.

As business demands a reliability that the old Internet does not provide, new networks are emerging – separate from, but inter-connected with the old – which offer specialised services that business subscribers are willing to pay for. We are already seeing this with subscription-based services provided by AOL, Prodigy and Microsoft Network.

Newer networks began to take embryonic shape in the early 1990s when it became apparent to businesses and governments alike that the 'Information Super Highway' of the future was not necessarily the Internet of the present. The telecommunications companies, in conjunction with major corporations and sometimes pump-primed with government subsidies, took up the challenge.

The emerging alternatives are distinguishable by their speed and reliability, and by the fact they charge higher prices than those levied by Internet

Access providers. MCI is building a network aimed at high performance for corporate users in the USA; @Home is the network focusing on using cable TV networks to deliver video to the home.

These developments could significantly raise the cost of Internet access and use in the future. But they should also assure that information will arrive safely, on time and in one piece.

14.4 Control and regulation

Answers to the problems of pirating and plagiarism are unlikely to be reached in the near future. The question of copyright is more likely to be resolved by the private sector through use of security mechanisms, appropriate pricing policies and seller-purchaser agreements, than through government controls.

According to a study commissioned for the European Parliament, pornography and racism are unlikely to be eradicated from the Internet, because such a move would require unprecedented and unacceptable levels of surveillance and limits to freedom of speech and action. Although it is possible to restrict undesirable Internet activities and access to them through technical solutions, action by Internet Service Providers and the weight of public opinion, it is virtually impossible to police the Internet in any concerted way.

But some help may be on the horizon. As the commercial networks emerge, the telecommunications companies are experimenting with new routing protocols in order to guarantee high performance. These include metering of who sends what, where, primarily in order to enable charging and taxation.

14.5 Bandwidth and data-switching

If Internet detractors have said that the Internet might collapse because its cable network will be unable to carry broadband into the home, they have reckoned without increasing numbers of developments and initiatives.

As we said in Chapter 3, fibre optics already form the telecommunications backbone in a growing number of countries, and the tentacles are beginning to reach out to the home and business alike.

Already the Internet can offer cheap – if not high quality – telephone services through packet-switching as opposed to direct connection. In January 1998, Memtel – part of Global eXchange, a US-based consortium – launched an Internet telephone service which can be used from any phone. Memtel plans to build Internet-based exchanges around the world in order to offer UK customers the significant savings on traditional telephone services to Europe, the USA and parts of Asia which American customers already receive.

But it is with the growth of cable TV that people will see speedy improvements to the quality of delivery. One estimate claims that over 10 million homes in the UK will have access to cable TV and therefore fibre optic lines in 1998. Fibre optic cable is also one of the foundations of the more robust, private networks being established by telecommunications companies which see information and entertainment services as the key to their future.

Fibre optics do not necessarily have a stranglehold on development potential as ISDN becomes more commonplace in business and, in a growing number of cases, is also reaching the home.

But there are also plans to push the Internet down ordinary electricity lines without the noise or corruption you might expect. Northern Telecom, a Canadian telecommunications equipment manufacturer and Norweb Communications, part of United Utilities, which operates energy and telecommunications businesses in the UK, are collaborating to offer commercial Internet trials in 1998 to 2,000 homes through standard electricity wires. If it works, it will create intense competition in the telecommunications industry.

Land-line cabling is not the only option as Microsoft in the USA and BT in the UK are among those exploring an Internet in the sky with satellite. Modem manufacturers have already produced plug-in cards to bring satellite services to the PC.

For those who don't, or won't, want to work with mouse-clicks and keyboards, telecommunications and software companies are preparing to offer the Internet on TV. TV-like push-button remote-control will replace the mouse and the keyboard, and the TV will offer home shopping, home banking and e-mail.

Some argue that the Internet is essentially about information and that TV is about entertainment; others that they are both about both. In order to display information services, the TV screen will need the fine resolution of PC monitors but NetSets (TV sets through which you can also access the Internet) are already on sale in the USA at affordable prices.

On top of all these initiatives, comes Internet2, a new super network with US government funding, being trialled where Internet1 started – in the American universities. Internet2 promises to be up to 1,000 times faster than the transmission speeds we currently experience, making rapid downloading of huge volumes of information a reality, along with advanced video-conferencing and 3-D movies. Internet2 will probably emerge as a development of, rather than a revolution from, Internet1, as the installation of high-speed routers begins to alleviate current congestion in information networking.

14.6 Addressing the future now

Addressing the future now means getting to grips with some strategic questions about which you will have to make some assumptions – or best guesses – or get left behind. These questions are about customers, technology and markets.

Customers

- How are demographics changing, and how will they continue to change in the next 20 years?
- How will national populations change in terms of power-groups, particularly the increase in the number of retired people and the growth of women in the workforce?
- How will life-styles change as populations shift, technologies improve and economies fluctuate or stabilise to impact on purchasing power?

Technology

- How long will it be before access to remote computers – via TVs or PCs, satellite or cable – is commonplace in the home?
- How long will it be before most large companies aggressively encourage teleworking?
- How long will it be before secure electronic payment methods

generate sufficient confidence for electronic commerce to take off?

- Will the combined technologies of Virtual Reality ('experience') and Inter-Relay Chat (interactivity) successfully allow the customer to test out products and services – try before you buy?

Markets

- Will advertisers be able to customise content and the timing of delivery to individuals as well as to communities? Will this be considered intrusive? Or, could it go horribly wrong as individuals' tastes and needs change outside the confines of predictable logic?
- With the consumer increasingly interacting with suppliers and producers, how long will it be before Alvin Toffler's 'pros-umer' (producers-consumers), predicted in 1980 in The Third Wave, become a widespread market phenomenon?
- Will the Internet change the current market relationship of supplier pushing to customer with the latter becoming pro-active and the supplier adopting a more responsive role? With the Internet enabling two-way communication, the customer can put out a request and then select from supplier offers received.

14.7 Managing in the future

How will managers adapt to using the Internet as it becomes more routine in all aspects of work?

We have compiled some ground-rules for managing in the future:

1. Information and knowledge are for sharing with customers, staff, even competitors and therefore the key to the organisation's development. Managers will have to work out what can be shared with whom and under what conditions.
2. Despite the continuing growth and availability of information, managers will need a capability for decision-making under uncertainty. There will never be enough information of exactly the right kind, so managers will still have to make an informed guess.

3 Managing uncertainty means motivating and controlling in a risk environment. It means encouraging the individual to take risks and initiatives at a time when job security has diminished and the outcome – due to the rise in competition – is less than sure.
4 Attaching importance to job security needs to be balanced with the recognition of the importance of learning, innovation and adaptability.
5 Learning means admitting that no-one will ever know it all (if they ever did). Fear of confessing ignorance will need replacing with an honest inquisitiveness.
6 Effective telecommunications means that working in remote locations can become the norm. Distance-working means that 'boss' and 'subordinate' do not see each other at regular times and that 'face-time' is no longer a measure of value (if it ever was).
7 Trust – in colleagues working at a distance and in new partners you have never met, or may never meet – will take on a new importance.
8 Managers will need to work out which kind of communication is best for each circumstance. With a choice between media such as the phone, e-mail, Web, meeting and written memo, efficient communication will be at a premium. Managers will need a keener perception of changing customer requirements and to know how to choose the appropriate communication medium to suit them.
9 Some futurists have predicted that intelligent gathering of customer requirements will make aggressive hard-sell a thing of the past. In the future the customer will buy, rather than be sold to.
10 As communication media and electronic functionality proliferate, cybermania of the future will need to be balanced with the cyberphobia of the past.

14.6 Managing yourself

In the beginning, the stereotypical user of the Internet, was referred to as a nerd, someone unable or unwilling to take a full and active part in society and who lived as fully as possible through the computer and who lacked certain interpersonal skills and capabilities. As the Internet develops into an effective business medium for the future, changing the way we work, we recognise that we cannot afford to become like that popular conception of the nerd. We need skills and capabilities including:

- an open mind and readiness to learn;
- adaptability to change;
- good time-management and ability to manage stress;
- genuine empathy with colleagues and customers;
- the ability to work on our own and in teams which are rapidly constructed and dissolved;
- a harmony with the ethical perspective and the social responsibility of the business;
- the ability to influence others by discussion, negotiation and persuasion;
- a knowledge of, and ability to pick out, good, reliable information sources;
- a commitment to recognising that we can all learn from whomsover, at whatsoever time;
- consistent judgement that is not afraid to make u-turns as change speeds up;
- a perspective on the broader picture and the ability to think strategically.

If the first phase of Internet development was dominated by the power of technology to change the way we do things, the next will test how we can adapt to that change and make it succeed.

Ironically, the very skills which early users of the Internet lacked, will be needed in abundance as it settles into an established method for doing business.

INDEX